12⁵⁰

D0732108

FRESH

Nourishing Salads for All Seasons

RECIPES AND PHOTOGRAPHS
KIMBERLY HARRIS

GENERAL EDITOR
JOEL HARRIS

Scooter Lane Publishing
Damascus, OR

Scooter Lane Publishing
Damascus, OR
www.thenourishinggourmet.com

ISBN 978-1-466-21389-0

To my husband- You are the reason that my life is tinted with yellows of sunshine, pinks of love, and greens of growth. I love you.

Contents

Introduction

With fruit salads to sweeten, side salads to complement, and main dish salads to nourish, there is a salad appropriate for every occasion. My Grandpa liked to say, "There is always room for salad." I agree. There should always be room on our menu for a variety of salads, as they are full of delicious and nourishing ingredients. Or at least they should be. Granted, there are plenty of recipes for home-made salads full of refined sugar, packets of seasoning, and highly refined oils. But making salads with old fashioned, good tasting, natural ingredients is just as easy and tastes better, too.

When I started planning this project, my number one priority was to make a book that I personally would want to use on a weekly basis – a book I would be willing to give space to in my own kitchen. So I did. My family and I enjoy all of the recipes in this book. Any recipe that we only moderately liked was eliminated. Of course, I included all of our favorite recipes that I've developed over the years. The result is a book full of recipes I want to serve to my family and guests on a regular basis. In short, a cookbook that I want for myself, and hope you'll want, too.

Many recipes are old classics, updated with fresh or more nourishing ingredients. Like a favorite pair of jeans, they are familiar and used often. Examples include *Caesar Salad*, *All American Potato Salad*, and the all time favorite, *Taco Salad*. Other recipes, while expanding the palate's horizon with new spices, flavors and ingredients, are still simple and easy to prepare.

I love experimenting with new ingredients and trying this or that bottle of oil and vinegar, but when push comes to shove, I want both my pantry and my recipes to be simple. I am not a full time chef. I am a busy mom and piano teacher and I maintain a food blog on top of it all. If I had to guess, I would say that you are busy, too, and therefore need to keep things simplified in the kitchen.

With that in mind, I've used only two vinegars for this entire book. I found that raw apple cider vinegar and balsamic vinegar were all that were necessary for the majority of recipes. You can make any of the recipes with a mild olive oil (though I sometimes provide other options as well). I've used one type of mustard (with the exception of the *American Potato Salad*), and minimized specialty ingredients whenever possible. What that translates into is recipes that are accessible and won't leave you running to the store for new ingredients every time you want to try a new recipe. With a few staples and fresh ingredients (such as lemons, herbs, and lettuce) you will be ready to bring satisfying salads to your table everyday.

As a side bonus to writing this book, eating all of the fresh produce while testing and re-testing my recipes boosted my energy and helped me be more focused. Who knew that writing a cookbook would actually help me get more accomplished in my everyday life? But that's what good food does for you. Here's to refreshing, good food. Enjoy!

Ingredients

It goes without saying that buying high quality ingredients is the first and most important step to making a high quality salad. Here's a quick run-through of the ingredients I recommend (be sure to also check out the Resource Section at the back of the book, pp. 124-125). I have limited the amounts called for on the higher cost items (seafood, organic meats, etc.) so that those of you who are budget-conscious like myself will find my recipes to be accessible, while still using superior ingredients.

Lettuce and Vegetables

Lettuce is one of the produce items I always try to buy organic since its delicate structure allows for more penetration of pesticides and other chemicals. There is a plethora of lettuce greens to explore, from the common green leaf lettuce and romaine, to the bitter chicory family with endive and radicchio. Other traditional greens are making a comeback in farmer's markets around the US. For my daily needs, I buy green/red leaf lettuce, romaine, and a spring salad mix (or a baby lettuce mix) at farmer's markets. I love the spiciness of watercress and arugula as well.

I encourage you to buy as many organic vegetables as possible, but if necessity dictates, at least avoid some of the most highly contaminated produce as listed in the "dirty dozen". This includes peaches, apples, celery, nectarines, strawberries, cherries, pears, grapes, spinach, lettuce and potatoes. I've found many local farmers who use organic, better than organic, or nearly organic practices but who aren't certified. They often have very affordable prices.

Extra Virgin Olive Oil & Other Oils

Late harvested olive oil has a buttery yellow color. For those accustomed to using refined oils, such as canola and other vegetable oils, a mild olive will greatly help in the transition to extra virgin olive oil. This is a transition I highly recommend you make, as canola oil and other vegetable oils are highly refined and contain a much too high omega 6 to 3 fatty acid ratio. On top of that, they are often made using genetically modified ingredients. One of my favorite mild olive oils is *Chaffin Family Orchards'* late harvest olive oil (www. chaffinfamilyorchards.com). I've also had success with other Californian small farm products.

For the gourmet, using an early harvest olive oil will contain more flavor (sometimes described as peppery or bitter). As an added bonus, it also contains more polyphenols and antioxidants. This is especially nice with the *Simple Balsamic Vinaigrette* (p. 118). Just don't use it to make homemade mayonnaise unless you really enjoy that peppery flavor. Most of the extra virgin olive oils you see in the store are a mix of different oils from different farmers, harvested both late and early.

When buying olive oil, I prefer brands that have a single source for their olive oil, as there has been much deception with adding inferior oils to "extra virgin olive oils". The more directly you can buy olive oil, the better. Buy in dark glass containers for best keep.

Other oils I use in this book include sesame oil, coconut oil, and toasted sesame oil. Cold-pressed sesame oil is a good source of vitamin E, is high in antioxidants and has a high smoke point. However, it does contain a higher amount of omega 6, so I wouldn't use it exclusively. Toasted sesame oil has a rich, dark flavor. It's used in my recipes for its beautiful flavor. Virgin, "raw", unrefined coconut oil is an excellent source of lauric acid, which has strong anti-fungal and antimicrobial properties. It is used in *"Mary's Oil Blend"* (p. 110). This blend can be used in any of the recipes.

Vinegar

The two vinegars used in this book are organic raw apple cider vinegar and balsamic vinegar. I love raw apple cider vinegar because it has all of the enzymes intact. Using raw vinegar such as raw apple cider vinegar may help you better digest the rest of your food. Raw apple cider vinegar is claimed to have many health benefits, but I personally think it just makes good sense to use a high quality vinegar that is as unprocessed as possible. When I first switched over, I was skeptical that I could make my salad dressing taste as good with it, but I was proved wrong. I hope this salad book proves the same to you. Look for brands that use the words "raw" and "unfiltered" when buying, such as *Solana Gold Apple Cider Vinegar* or *Bragg's Apple Cider Vinegar*.

The second vinegar I use is organic balsamic vinegar. It has a sweet rich flavor that is unsurpassed. The longer it has been aged, the sweeter and thicker it becomes. In testing I used *Bionaturae*

Organic Balsamic Vinegar for my "everyday" balsamic, and *Napa Valley Naturals, Grand Reserve Vinegar* (aged up to 18 years) for a very sweet dressing.

Mustard

I've used a variety of mustards in my kitchen, but when it came to writing this book I knew I wanted to test all of my recipes with a mustard I could stand behind. I found that in *Eden's Organic Brown Mustard*. I've found it to be an excellent multi-purpose mustard. It comes in a glass jar and the ingredients are simple: "Organic whole mustard seed, organic apple cider vinegar, water, Eden sea salt". However, a Dijon style mustard also works well and many of my recipe testers used Dijon when testing my recipes with excellent results. I would recommend buying organic, as the vinegar in many (if not most) mustards contains genetically modified ingredients.

Unrefined Salt

Unrefined salt is unbleached and full of its natural nutrients. It is a completely different product when compared to bleached, refined, whiter-than-your-teeth table salt. Good brands include *Real Salt*, and *Celtic Sea Salt*. Your taste buds will thank you for making the switch.

Honey

I've almost exclusively used honey to sweeten the recipes in this book. I do use other unrefined sweeteners in my kitchen, but I found that honey works best for salad dressings. It doesn't overly flavor dressing (like a whole cane sugar, such as rapadura, often would) and works well for both fruit salads and savory salad dressings. I prefer to use raw, unfiltered honey when not heating it. You can heat raw honey until it's just liquefied to help with blending it into other ingredients, but it should never be warmed above body temperature if you want to keep the enzymes in the honey alive.

Seafood

I've sought to use sustainable, low mercury seafood in my recipes. I've found the Monterey Bay Aquarium's guidelines helpful in this regard. I use Oregon caught, wild pink shrimp, Wild Alaskan salmon, low mercury canned tuna from the company *Wild Planet*, and farmed Washington clams (farmed right in their natural environment). Look up the best choices for your area, or buy high quality frozen seafood.

Beef & Dairy

The majority of the beef I use is 100% grassfed beef I buy in a "cow share" from local farmers and keep in my freezer. Grassfed beef has a much higher omega 3 content and also contains CLA (conjugated linoleic acid). CLA has shown in studies to have an anti-cancer effect, reduce fat, build lean muscle, and promote anti-atherosclerotic activity. For these reasons, some have even begun to call grassfed beef a "superfood". Grassfed dairy is also much higher in nutrients, so I try to find grassfed dairy whenever possible.

Since my daughter and I are sensitive to cheese made from cow's milk, we have found goat cheese to be wonderful in salads. You can use either in my recipes.

Chicken & Eggs

The very best chicken and chicken eggs are bought from local farmers who pasture their chickens, allowing them to eat plenty of bugs and greens from their natural environment. The chicken will have a richer, fuller flavor, as well as being a purer product. The eggs will have rich, golden yolks. After pastured, organic, free range chicken and chicken eggs are the next best choice. If you can find and afford them, I highly recommend it.

Beans

I love beans in salads. I have converted several of my friends to the practice of adding a cupful of cooked beans to a green salad. It is a simple and frugal way to "up" the protein content of a salad.

You may use canned beans in my recipes (I recommend that you keep some cans on hand for last minute meals). However, canned goods do contain BPA, a known toxin that you especially want to avoid with young children, and pregnant and nursing mothers.

Eden's canned beans are canned in BPA-free cans and are cooked with kombu, a seaweed that makes the beans more digestible and tasty. They are more expensive, so I keep a couple of Eden's canned beans in my pantry, and try to cook most of my beans myself. You will find my directions for homemade beans on p. 115. Making your own beans is by far the cheapest option.

Nuts

Once again, nuts bought from farmers who treat their trees well (no pesticides and good soil care) will give you a higher quality product both in taste and purity. However, most of the pesticide will not affect the nutmeat directly when trees are treated. If you can't find or afford the very best, you can rest assured that nuts are not likely to be highly contaminated.

I like to pan toast all of the nuts I use. This brings out a richer flavor in the nuts, and since it evaporates some of the moisture, it gives them a nice crunch. A simple and tasty way to consume your nuts!

Nuts kept in the freezer can keep for up to 8 months, or 4 months in the refrigerator. Toss nuts if they smell rancid and be sure to purchase them within the "use by" date.

Practical Tips

To Emulsify Your Dressing

You don't need any special containers for making salad dressing, unless you want something pretty. All you really need is a Mason jar and a lid. With a quick vigorous shake, your dressing will be emulsified, and you can easily store the leftovers in the refrigerator. However, you may want to buy plastic storing lids made for Mason jars as they won't corrode over time from having vinegar splashed on them.

Warming Solidified Dressing

Be aware that the olive oil in your dressing will solidify when cold. To warm, place in a bowl and run warm water over the jar until the dressing has liquefied again. Or, shake vigorously until the motion warms the dressing enough to liquefy.

To Wash Your Lettuce

Organic lettuce may have a few bugs on it. Glory in it, as that means it really is organic. However, you do want to wash it well to remove any dirt and/or bugs.

Treat delicate lettuce kindly. For delicate heads of lettuce, such as butter leaf, run water over each individual leaf and then place in a bowl or salad spinner (I use one without holes on the bottom) and cover with water. Swish the lettuce around and drain. Repeat once or twice if the lettuce is especially dirty or sandy. Spin in the salad spinner to dry, or pat dry with clean towels or paper towels. Store in a salad bag (see below), or in plastic bags or containers along with a clean kitchen towel or a few paper towels to wick any extra moisture off.

For less delicate lettuce, such as romaine, I've found the following method to be a time saver: Place the unwashed lettuce on a cutting board and cut off the stem. Slice into half inch pieces. Place the lettuce in a bowl or salad spinner and cover with water. Swish the lettuce around and drain. Cover with water once or twice more, depending on how dirty the lettuce is. Dry and store as listed above.

For spring mixes, baby arugula, or spinach, wash even if the package says "prewashed".

If you keep washed and dried salad in the refrigerator, along with one or two pre-made dressings, you will always be ready to throw together a quick green salad.

Using a Salad Bag

I recently discovered "salad bags" made out of microfiber cloth for a very absorbent material. This removes the need for either a salad spinner or plastic bags to store your lettuce in. Simple wash your lettuce in a bowl, drain and stick right into the bag while still damp. I've had success using salad bags to store my greens, with just slight problems with wilting on the top layer of salad greens.

Tossing Your Salad

You will want to gently toss your salad to prevent bruising. The very best way is to toss with your clean bare hands. Practically speaking, this is not the most kosher way to toss a salad in front of a table full of guests, but in a private kitchen, it's certainly the easiest way. Otherwise, use wooden tongs and gently toss all of the ingredients until just combined.

There is nothing more frustrating than having your salad bowl continually overflow and spill onto the countertops when tossing a salad. I've found that the best practice is to toss a large salad in a very large bowl (the largest you own), and then transfer into a serving bowl or platter for presentation.

To Serve

We think of salads as always being served in bowls, but you can also serve them on lovely platters. Toss first in a large bowl, as instructed above, and then artfully display on a platter. For a pretty presentation, you can hold back some of the ingredients, such as chicken, toasted nuts, herbs, etc, to sprinkle over top the tossed salad.

For some of the side vegetable salads, I've found that they look beautiful in large personal pasta bowls (a cross between a plate and a bowl), smaller platters, and medium sized pottery bowls. For family, we often keep it as simple as can be. But it's nice to present your salad in a pretty way when serving to guests or for special family meals. (I think it makes it taste better, too!)

For a Picnic or Potluck

Most green salads will wilt after an hour or two in the dressing, so when bringing a salad somewhere such as a picnic or potluck, you don't want to toss the salad before you leave. If you've used a Mason jar to make your dressing, it's easy to bring along. Or, if you would rather, pour the appropriate amount of dressing on the bottom of a serving bowl, and then layer the rest of the ingredients over it (with the greens last). When ready to serve, it's a simple as tossing everything together in the one bowl.

On a Hot Day

It is very disappointing to find your plate of salad wilted on a hot day when you were especially hoping for a refreshing meal. To keep the lettuce cool, don't set out your salad bowl too early, and serve on chilled plates (simply stick the plates in the freezer for ten minutes before serving).

Your Own "House" Salad

Every good restaurant has a house salad and salad dressing. They are generally made out of simple, everyday ingredients tossed with a widely appealing salad dressing. I think every household should have their own "house" salad, too. It should be a salad that appeals directly to your particular household, and that you would like to eat weekly or even daily. Your house salad can have two versions: a simple side salad to go with your main dish, or a main dish salad plumped up with protein and served with a side of bread.

Here are a few tips:
1. None of the ingredients should be extremely expensive, unless you have a generous food budget. There are some salads that would be lovely to eat everyday, but unpractical for most budgets.
2. It shouldn't be difficult or time consuming to make. If your house salad is going to be consumed on a regular basis, it should be simple to throw together.
3. It should include some of your favorite ingredients, whether tomatoes, feta cheese, olives, black beans or chicken. It should also use your favorite dressing.
4. Keep washed and dried lettuce ready for use in the refrigerator along with your favorite homemade dressing, and you will always be ready to whip together your house salad.

If you are new to making your own dressing, then I would encourage you to try out some of my recipes to get a feel for what you like best. Perhaps you will like my personal "house" dressing, the *Everyday Salad Dressing* (p. 118), or perhaps you will find that you are more of a *Simple Balsamic Vinaigrette* (p. 118) household. Experiment to find out what you like best. Flip through the Salad Dressing section (pp. 118-123) and see what sounds good to you.

Other ingredients that you can toss in include: cooked beans such as black beans, white beans, or chickpeas; canned salmon or canned low mercury tuna; shredded cheddar cheese, crumbled bleu, feta, or gorgonzola cheese; tomatoes, olives, cucumbers, carrots, red cabbage for a bit of color, toasted nuts or seeds, shredded leftover chicken or beef, and so on. The sky is the limit!

Have fun exploring what works best for you, and once you've settled on your own "house" salad, change it up a bit every once in a while to include seasonal ingredients as well.

How to Use this Book

Mix and Match

Most of the dressings will be found in the last chapter of the book. I formatted the recipes this way as you can mix and match the salad recipes to the salad dressing recipes. I've included suggested alternative dressings for many of the salads. Have fun playing around with the combinations.

Serving Sizes

Serving sizes are tricky. One person may eat 3 servings at one sitting. Another, who served the dish with plenty of other dishes or courses, may only eat a half of a serving. I decided to give suggested numbers of how many a recipe should serve. Of course, this varies as well. And my recipe testers were no help! One family said that my recipe served more than my suggested serving, while another said it served less!

All in all, take my serving numbers as suggestions and figure out what works best for you.

Inspiration

I hope that this book will provide you with many recipes that you will want to use often. But I also hope that you use this book to inspire you to create your own unique salads using what you have on hand. Salads are like soups in that they are easily adaptable to what is available and on hand. I felt like with every recipe I came up with, ten new ideas would pop into my head. Salad options are endless!

Enjoy!

Classic Salads

Nourishing Caesar Salad

Fresh Taco Salad

All American Potato Salad

Wilted Spinach Salad with Hot Bacon Dressing

Salad Lyonnaise

Greek Salad

Leon Salad

Salmon Ceviche

In this section you will find salads that are well known and loved by many. Several of these salads are actually based off of restaurant salads. For example, Caesar Salad was originally served at a restaurant owned by Caesar Cardini (hence the name). Leon Salad is still served today at La Scala in Beverly Hills. The following recipes are my own take on these classics.

Other salads include a wilted bacon and spinach salad, a ceviche which has roots that travel far back into history, and an all American potato salad– a beloved American tradition. Of course, all of these recipes use pure, natural ingredients for a nourishing salad.

These are salads that are often served at home and shared with others. I would happily eat all of these salads on a weekly basis, as I love them all.

Nourishing Caesar Salad

Caesar salad is a cinch to make with homemade dressing, grated parmesan cheese, and plenty of romaine lettuce. A well loved salad, Caesar salad is here to stay. With the nutrient dense dressing, this is a satisfying and nourishing salad as well. This version has chicken, but for a side salad, feel free to leave it off.

* * * Serves 4-6 Main Dish Salads, 8-10 Side Dish Salads * * *

1 large head of romaine lettuce (washed & dried, torn/cut into bite sized pieces, about 8-12 cups worth)
1/2 to 3/4 cup of freshly grated Parmesan cheese
1 recipe of Roasted Chicken or Sautéed Chicken, pp. 106-108
1 recipe of Herbed Garlic Croutons, p. 109
1 recipe of Caesar Salad Dressing, p. 119

1. Make the salad dressing, herbed croutons, and chicken.

2. Place the romaine lettuce, chicken, and croutons in a large bowl. Toss with Caesar Salad Dressing. Sprinkle with Parmesan cheese and serve.

Dairy Free Version: Caesar salad can be hard to create dairy free, but my dairy free friend and I found that substituting the **Double Roasted Garlic Dressing, p. 120**, and leaving off the shredded cheese gave a close parallel.

I didn't know the history of Caesar Salad until I was writing this book. It is accredited to Caesar Cardini, an Italian born Mexican who created it for his restaurant. It's since become one of the most recognized salads in our country, with family restaurants and five-star restaurants alike serving their own versions.

You could vary this salad by topping it with seafood, such as shrimp, or even sliced pan roasted grassfed steak, p. 104.

Fresh Taco Salad

This salad is a crowd pleaser and a sure winner at my house. We've made it for both family meals and large parties. I grew up eating taco salad, but this is my updated version, complete with creamy dressings (two choices) and flavorful meat without a seasoning packet. With a creamy dressing, crunchy chips, and flavorful meat and vegetables, this salad is the full meal deal. It is easily adaptable to your favorite flavor combination. Keep it simple, if desired, or add a variety of Mexican themed ingredients. Both dressing choices are excellent.

* * * SERVES 4-6 MAIN DISH SALADS * * *

For the Salad:
1 medium head of romaine lettuce, or two hearts or romaine, washed, dried and torn/cut into bite sized pieces (8-12 cups)
1 recipe of Mexican Ground Beef, p. 105
1-2 large avocados, peeled and cut into bite sized pieces
1 1/2 cups of cooked black beans (homemade, p. 115)
1 small bunch of cilantro, washed, stemmed and chopped
1 cup of sliced black olives
Several handfuls of crumbled corn chips (preferably organic)
2 large tomatoes, stemmed and diced

Other Optional Additions:
1 cup of shredded cheddar cheese (preferably grassfed and raw)
1 red bell pepper, seeded and chopped

Salad Dressing:
Creamy Mexican Avocado Dressing, p. 122, or
1 cup of canned organic salsa mixed with 1 cup of additive free organic sour cream until well combined.

Tossed Taco Salad
1. Make the salad dressing and Mexican Ground Beef. Prepare the vegetables.

2. Place the lettuce in a very large bowl. Add the rest of the ingredients for the salad, including the Mexican Ground Beef, slightly cooled.

3. Toss with the dressing of choice and serve. (The dressing, being a little gloppy, may not be the prettiest, but it's certainly delicious).

Make Your Own Taco Salad
Arrange all of the ingredients separately in bowls with serving spoons, with the lettuce placed at the start of the "line". The dressing can be simply dolloped on top and individually mixed in with the salad ingredients.

All American Potato Salad

I can't pass up the opportunity to share a recipe for an old favorite, American Potato Salad. This version is my absolute favorite. If you like your potato salad a bit less tangy, cut down on the vinegar. For added crunch, add two celery sticks, finely diced.

* * * SERVES 6-8 * * *

3 pounds of red potatoes (peeled or skin left on), diced into 1 to 1 1/2 inch pieces
2 tablespoons unrefined salt
1/4 cup of raw apple cider vinegar
4-6 eggs
1 cup of mayonnaise, homemade, p. III, (see resource section, p. 125, for purchased mayonnaise recommendations)
2 tablespoons raw apple cider vinegar
1 teaspoon dill weed
1 1/2 teaspoons celery seed
2 tablespoons yellow mustard
1/4 cup of pickle relish (I recommend Bubbie's Pickle Relish)

1. Put the diced potatoes into a large pot and just cover with cool water. Add 2 tablespoons of unrefined salt. Bring to a boil, then turn down heat and simmer for about 7 minutes, or until the potatoes are just tender. Drain in a colander. Sprinkle with 1/4 cup of apple cider vinegar and let cool.

2. Put the eggs into a medium pot, cover with water, and cover pan with a lid. Bring to a low boil, and then remove immediately from heat. Let sit in the hot water for 15 minutes, then drain and rinse with cold water to cool. Peel and dice.

3. Combine the mayonnaise, dill weed, celery seed, 2 tablespoons of vinegar and mustard in a bowl and whisk to combine. Stir in the pickle relish.

4. Combine the potatoes, eggs and sauce in a serving bowl and gently combine. Chill before serving. Can make 24 hours in advance.

To Peel or not to Peel?
There are more nutrients in the peels of potatoes, but if there is any green beneath the skin of the potato, you should peel it. The green layer indicates that an alkaloid, called solanine, may be present. Solanine is toxic. It would take many green potatoes to make you sick, but a hearty serving of potato salad made using potatoes with green under their skin could give you a nasty stomachache.

Wilted Spinach Salad with Hot Bacon Dressing

In this salad, a hot bacon dressing is poured over spinach, making it partially wilt. It's a delicious method. I keep this salad simple most of the time, but sliced boiled eggs or mushrooms are also a great addition. You can also use young dandelion leaves (bought at some stores or gathered wild from areas not sprayed) to replace the spinach. They are slightly bitter, and don't wilt much at all, but delicious nevertheless.

* * * 4-6 SIDE DISH SALADS * * *

1/2-3/4 pound baby spinach, washed and dried
6 slices of bacon, nitrate free
2 shallots, diced
1 tablespoon brown mustard (Eden's Organic Brown
   Mustard or Dijon style mustard)
1/3 cup of apple cider vinegar
2 teaspoons unrefined, whole cane sugar, maple
   sugar, or coconut sugar
Unrefined salt and freshly ground pepper, if needed

1. Place the spinach in a large bowl.

2. In a large saucepan, cook the bacon over medium heat, flipping frequently, untill well done and crispy. Remove to cool. Once cooled, crumble the bacon over the spinach.

3. Keep 1/4 to 1/3 cup of bacon grease in the pan and add the chopped shallot. Cook for 1 to 2 minutes, until just softened. Add the mustard, vinegar, and sugar. If not simmering already, bring to a simmer. Pour over spinach. Toss and serve.

Spinach is full of vitamins, such as vitamin K, A, and C, as well as magnesium and calcium, making it a great dark green to consume.

However, one caution is in order. Spinach contains a substance called <u>oxalic acid which actually blocks you from absorbing calcium and iron. It may also be associated with kidney stones.</u> This means that you probably don't want to depend on spinach for calcium or iron, and I would also caution you from eating raw spinach everday. <u>Cooking removes most of the oxalic acid.</u>

Salad Lyonnaise: Poached Egg Salad with Bacon and Croutons

Salad Lyonnaise is a popular salad in France, and for good reason. It's a magical combination of frisée (otherwise known as curly endive, a slightly bitter lettuce), bacon, croutons and poached egg. This is my version. I don't always have frisée on hand, but I've found that I enjoy this with a good spring mix of young lettuces, especially if it contains flavorful, more bitter lettuce leaves. This is the one salad in this book that you will need to individually plate. Because it is as easy to make for one person, or a group of 8, I've given directions for what you'll need per plate.

* * *

Per Plate:

About 2 cups of young salad mix, or frisée lettuce, washed and dried (if using frisée, tear into bite sized pieces)

1-2 slices of nitrate free bacon

1 small slice of bread, cubed (sourdough, sprouted wheat, gluten free, etc.)

1 egg (the fresher the better for poached eggs – they will hold together better)

2 teaspoons raw apple cider vinegar, optional

2-3 tablespoons vinaigrette of choice

1. In a large saucepan, cook the bacon over medium heat, flipping frequently, until crispy and cooked through. Remove from pan. Once cooled, crumble.

2. In the hot bacon grease, add your cubed bread. Flip to cook on both sides. (It takes just a minute or two on each side). You can add more fat (such as butter) if needed when making a single serving. Remove from pan.

3. In a smaller saucepan, heat several inches of water with the optional vinegar (it will help hold the eggs together, omit if you don't like the added vinegar taste). Crack the eggs right into the water and simmer for 3 to 4 minutes for runny yolks. Remove with a slotted spoon to a plate lined with a paper towel.

4. Toss the salad greens with the dressing of choice and plate. Top with the bacon, croutons and egg. Serve.

I buy nitrate free bacon at the meat counter at my local store, New Seasons Market. They make it themselves using a simple sugar and salt brine, without added nitrates. Most organic nitrate free bacons use a celery juice, or celery juice powder, a natural source of nitrates. Bacon cured without any nitrates will not be as pink in color. Nitrate free bacon does burn more easily. After cooking it for years, I've discovered that cooking at a lower temperature and flipping the bacon frequently helps cook it evenly without burning it. Just make sure to keep a close eye on it!

Greek Salad

Salty cheese and olives, fresh cucumbers, tomatoes and lettuce, and a bright lemon-based salad dressing, how can you go wrong? Because we don't do a lot of cow dairy, I have used goat cheese feta in this recipe and we all loved it. However, both work wonderfully.

* * * SERVES 4-6 MAIN DISH SALADS, 8-10 SIDE DISH SALADS * * *

1 head of romaine lettuce, washed, dried and
  thinly sliced (about 8-12 cups worth)
1/2 pound of feta cheese (cow or goat), cubed or
  crumbled into bite sized pieces
1 large red pepper, stemmed, seeded and cubed or
  thinly sliced
1/2 to 1 red onion, peeled and thinly sliced
About 1 cup of kalamata olives or Greek black
  olives, cut in half
2-4 medium tomatoes, cut into wedges
1 large cucumber, peeled, if desired, and thinly
  sliced
Lemon pepper dressing with garlic and oregano,
  p. 119

Wash, chop and assemble all of the above ingredients. Make dressing. Place the lettuce in a large bowl and combine with the rest of the ingredients. Toss with dressing. Serve.

Greek salad obviously pairs well with Greek main dishes and sides, such as avgolemono, gyros, and roast lamb. But it also goes nicely with many meats (think grilled steak or chicken), sandwiches, and soups.

I prefer this Greek salad with lettuce, even though originally, it didn't contain any. It is often served with a vinaigrette, but I like how the lemon dressing lightens the salty ingredients.

Leon Salad

My sister-in-law made vast bowlfuls of Leon salad to serve to the Harris crowd last summer. We all enjoyed the lovely flavor combination. This is my version of the famous salad, which was originally and still is served at La Scala in Beverly Hills. The combination of salami, black olives and chickpeas enhanced with fresh basil is amazing. I also love how quick this salad is to throw together. Because most salamis have nitrates in them, I buy Applegate's delicious organic Genoa salami from my local health food store. It's delicious in this salad.

* * * SERVES 4-6 MAIN DISH SALADS, 8-10 SIDE DISH SALADS * * *

I head of romaine lettuce, or two romaine hearts, washed, dried and thinly sliced (about 8-12 cups worth)

1/4 pound of thinly sliced salami cut into 1/2 inch pieces

1/4 pound thinly sliced provolone, cut into 1/2 inch pieces, optional (you can replace with more salami)

I to I 1/2 cup of black olives thinly sliced

8 ounces of cherry tomatoes, halved

I cup of basil, washed, dried, torn or cut into small pieces

I 1/2 cups of chickpeas, homemade (p. 115) or canned, drained and rinsed if canned

1/2 or I red onion, thinly sliced

3/4 cup to I cup of Everyday Salad Dressing, p. 118 or Lemon Pepper Dressing with Garlic & Basil, p. 119

1. Place the prepared lettuce in a large bowl. As you chop and slice the rest of the ingredients, add right into the bowl.

2. When ready to serve, toss with desired dressing and serve right away.

Salmon Ceviche

Ceviche is a long used method of preparing seafood which was most likely originated in Peru. Fish (or shrimp and shellfish) is marinated in citrus juice until the fish firms up and has a cooked texture. In this version, the fish is then drained and tossed with many flavorful, Mexican based ingredients, creating a wonderful salad. It's so simple too! You can also serve this with corn chips or as a taco filling. It's now recommended that you freeze fish for 7 days before eating raw to kill any parasites. Using the lemon and lime juice cuts down on any bacteria, meaning that this dish is much safer to eat than sushi, especially if frozen beforehand.

* * * SERVES 4-6 SMALL SERVINGS * * *

12 ounces of salmon, deboned, skinned and cut into small pieces*

1/3 cup of fresh lime juice

1/3 cup of fresh lemon juice

1 small avocado, peeled and diced

1 grapefruit, skin cut off and cut into bite sized pieces

1 small red pepper or half of a large red pepper, stemmed, seeded and cut into bite sized pieces

Small handful of cilantro (about 1/2 cup chopped)

1 Anaheim pepper, stemmed and chopped

Plenty of unrefined salt

1. Place the salmon in a medium sized bowl and cover with the lime and lemon juice. The salmon should be completely covered. Place in the refrigerator for about 4 hours (no longer than 6). Remove salmon with a slotted spoon and place in a serving bowl.

2. Add all of the vegetables and the rest of the ingredients to the salmon. Salt to taste (you will need plenty to balance the lime marinade) and serve.

*To debone fish, run a knife over the surface of the fish to feel where the bones are protruding. They should hit the knife at about half inch intervals. Using pliers, pull the bones out. I find it easiest to buy fish that's already been deboned.

*To skin the salmon, put the salmon skin side down on a cutting board. Place a very sharp knife right above the skin and carefully cut the skin off with the knife slightly angled downwards towards the skin.

Mains & Sides

Mexican Squash & Black Bean Salad

Steak & Arugula Salad

Everyday Autumn & Cranapple Walnut Salad

Simple Salmon Salad

Bacon, Egg, & Avocado Salad

Endive & Pear Salad

Watercress, Avocado, & Grapefruit Salad

Arugula, Grape & Chicken Salad

Holiday Salad: Candied Nuts, Pears & Blue Cheese

Strawberry & Goat Cheese Salad

Summertime Peach & Chicken Salad

Bowls full of leafy greens are what comes to mind when I think of the word "salad". This section. along with the Classic Salad Section is the main thrust of the book. (though the other sections contain many more favorites of mine).

Sometimes I just toss some greens with my favorite dressing and serve it as a simple side. Other times, it's the focal point of the meal with added meat, nuts, and other vegetables. I recommend serving plenty of bread and butter on the side with a main dish salad, especially for hearty eaters.

Many of these recipes can be either sides or main dishes. When served as a side salad, they serve many more people. The protein components are optional for side salads.

Estimating how many persons each recipe will feed is tricky. If you are like me and my husband, you can polish off far more than one serving size of a green salad. But others have smaller appetites, or children. Take my yield as a suggestion. The lower numbers for heartier eaters.

Mexican Squash & Black Bean Salad

This flavorful salad uses two Mexican ingredients, squash and black beans, as the centerpiece.
Cilantro, avocado and sweet pepper back up the Mexican theme and pumpkin seeds add a nice crunch.
It is a delicious and refreshing salad. I especially love the sweetness of the cooked squash in this salad.
For even more flavor you could add a soft, Mexican cheese, such as queso fresco.

* * * Serves 4-6 Main Dish Salads, 8-10 Side Salads * * *

One 2-3 pound butternut squash, peeled, seeded and cut into cubes

2 tablespoons olive oil or Mary's Oil Blend, p. 110

1 teaspoon ground cumin

1/8 teaspoon of cayenne

2-3 garlic cloves, minced or put through a garlic press

Unrefined Salt

1 head of lettuce, washed, dried, and cut/torn into bite sized pieces (8-12 cups)

3 cups of cooked black beans (homemade, p. 115)

1/2 to 1 cup of pumpkin seeds

1/2 bunch of cilantro, washed and finely minced

1 sweet bell pepper, seeded, stemmed and cubed

1 large avocado, peeled and cubed

1 recipe of Mexican Vinaigrette, p. 123

1. Preheat the oven to 425 degrees Fahrenheit. Place the cubed squash on a pan (you may want to use two pans, if the squash is crowded) and drizzle with oil. Sprinkle with the cumin, garlic and cayenne and thoroughly salt. Mix with your hands right on the pan and spread out evenly, leaving plenty of empty space. Cook for 35 to 45 minutes, or until the squash is soft and starting to brown around the edges. Allow to cool slightly before tossing with the rest of the ingredients.

2. In a small saucepan, toast the pumpkin seeds over medium high heat, stirring as needed to prevent burning and to brown evenly, until the seeds are lightly browned. Remove to cool on a plate.

3. In a large bowl, add the lettuce, black beans, cilantro, sweet bell pepper, avocado, pumpkin seeds, and squash. Toss with the Mexican Vinaigrette and serve.

Alternative Dressing:
Creamy Mexican Avocado Dressing, p. 122

✳ Steak & Arugula Salad

Juicy tomato and grass fed steak tops a bed of flavorful arugula and mild zucchini. The sweet balsamic vinaigrette tames the arugula and adds wonderful flavor to the tomato, zucchini and steak. This is a great salad to serve meat lovers. It's also a more frugal way to enjoy your steak. Enjoy!

* * * SERVES 2-4 MAIN DISH SALADS * * *

One 12 ounce steak such as sirloin, pan roasted
   and thinly sliced, p. 104
5 ounces of baby arugula, washed and dried well,
   or one bunch of mature arugula, washed and
   dried thoroughly.
1 medium zucchini, thinly sliced or cut into
   matchsticks
4 ounces of grape tomatoes, halved, or 1
   large tomato thinly cut
About 3/4 cup of Simple Balsamic Vinaigrette,
   p. 118

1. Cook the sirloin steak as directed on p. 104. While it is resting, cut up the vegetables and place them with the arugula in a large serving bowl.

2. Toss with vinaigrette (about 1/2 to 3/4 of a cup). Serve.

Alternative Dressing:
Creamy Mexican Avocado Dressing, p. 122
Roasted Garlic Dressing, or Double Garlic Dressing, p. 120

Arugula, also known as "rocket", has a peppery flavor. I love it with balsamic as the sweetness of the vinegar balances the strong flavor of the arugula.

While I am not always a raw zucchini fan, this is one of the recipes I love it in. Of course, the salad is almost as good without it, but the zucchini adds another flavor and texture dimension as well as nutrients. One recipe tester added feta cheese to this recipe and loved the extra addition.

Two Fall Salads: Everyday Autumn & Cranapple Walnut

Both of these salads are favorites around here. I make the Everyday Autumn Salad often, and the Cranapple Walnut Salad is a treat. Both are also quite simple, and both serve 10 side salads. If you make the Everyday Autumn Salad a main dish salad it will serve 4-6.

Everyday Autumn Salad

1 head of lettuce (green or red leaf, romaine, or butterleaf), washed, dried and torn into bite sized pieces, or about 8-12 cups of baby lettuce mix

2-3 crisp apples, cored and diced

1/2 to 3/4 cup of pumpkin seeds (can substitute walnuts, if desired)

3/4 to 1 cup of Everyday Salad Dressing, p. 118

1. In a small saucepan toast the pumpkin seeds over medium high heat until they are lightly toasted, stirring as needed to evenly brown and prevent burning.

2. In a large bowl, combine the lettuce, diced apples, pumpkin seeds, and the optional main dish ingredients.

3. Toss with dressing and serve.

For Main Dish Salad add one or both of the following:

2 cups of Gorgonzola or blue cheese (about 1/2 a pound)

1 recipe of Roasted Chicken Breast or Sautéed Chicken, pp. 106-108

Alternative Dressings: Simple Balsamic Vinaigrette, p. 118, Roasted Garlic Dressing (or Double Garlic Dressing), p. 120

Cranapple Walnut Salad

10 cups of baby lettuce mix, or 1 head of lettuce of choice, washed, dried and torn/cut into bite sized pieces

1 cup of dried cranberries (fruit juice sweetened)

1 large apple or 2 small, washed and diced *pear*

1 to 2 cups of walnuts or Cinnamon Vanilla Candied Nuts, p. 113

3/4 to 1 cup of salad dressing such as Simple Balsamic Dressing, p. 118, Sweet Apple Cider Vinaigrette, p. 121, or Everyday Salad Dressing, p. 118 *add cranberry sauce to dressing*

1. If using plain walnuts, toast walnuts in a medium sized pan over medium high heat until the walnuts are slightly browned and fragrant. Stir as needed to prevent burning and evenly toast. Remove to a plate and set aside to cool. Once cool, chop into 1/2 inch pieces, if desired.

2. In a large bowl, combine the lettuce, cranberries, apple and walnuts. Toss with desired dressing and serve.

✳ *Simple Salmon Salad*

Once I was running late on making dinner before my husband and I needed to leave for a meeting. I opened a can of salmon, toasted some nuts, and tossed them together with some lettuce I had washed previously and my pre-made salad dressing. It only took five minutes to make, but we sat down to a meal that was delicious! We loved the salad so much that I make it often for us now (both with canned and freshly cooked salmon). Simple goodness. Serve with buttered toast or crusty artisan bread.

* * * SERVES 4-6 MAIN DISH SALADS * * *

1 head of lettuce, washed, dried and cut/torn into
   bite sized pieces (8-12 cups)
About 2-3 cups of leftover cooked salmon or
   canned salmon, drained
1 cup of walnuts or slivered and blanched
   almonds
1 small or 1/2 large red onion, peeled and thinly
   sliced or chopped
3/4 to 1 cup of Simple Balsamic Vinaigrette, p. 118

1. In a dry pan over medium high heat, toast the nuts until they are browned and fragrant, stirring as needed for even browning. Remove to a plate to cool. If using walnuts, chop if desired.

2. In a serving bowl combine the lettuce, salmon, nuts and red onion. Toss with Simple Balsamic Dressing and serve.

Salmon is my favorite source of omega 3 fatty acids. Make sure you buy wild salmon (I recommend Alaskan). I love Wild Planet's Wild Alaskan canned salmon for its taste, quality, and the BPA-free cans.

This salad is also very tasty with part or all of the lettuce replaced with arugula (one of my personal favorites).

Other suggestions: Add sliced celery for added crunch or fresh herbs (such as basil) for even more flavor.

Bacon, Egg, & Avocado Salad

*This is a popular salad in my household. Rich, but refreshing, it makes
a satisfying salad in any season. It's very simple as well as easily adaptable.*

* * * Serves 4-6 Main Dish Salads, 8-10 Side Salads * * *

1 medium sized head of lettuce washed, dried and
  torn/cut into bite sized pieces (8-12 cups of
  bite sized pieces)
6-8 thick cut bacon slices, nitrate free
6 eggs
2 large avocados, peeled, seeded and cubed
1 large tomato, stemmed and diced, optional
3/4 to 1 cup of Everyday Salad Dressing, p. 118

Optional Additions:
Herbed Garlic Croutons, p. 109
Juicy Grassfed Steak, p. 104
Roasted Chicken or Sautéed Chicken, p. 106-108

1. Place eggs in a medium sized pan and cover with cool
water, and cover. Bring to a boil. Take off of the heat and let
sit, covered for 15 minutes. Drain and rinse with cold water.
Peel and cube.

2. In the meantime, in a large saucepan, fry the bacon over
medium heat, turning frequently until cooked through and
crispy. Cook in batches if needed. Cool and crumble.

3. Combine the lettuce, bacon, eggs, tomato, and avocado in
a bowl and toss with the Everyday Salad Dressing. Serve right
away.

Alternative Dressings:
Mexican Avocado Dressing, p. 122
Simple Balsamic Vinaigrette, p. 118

To Cube an Avocado
*Cut the avocado in half and
twist to separate. Remove the pit
(I use a spoon). Using a sharp
paring knife, cube directly in
the peel, being careful not to cut
through the peel to your hand.*

*Using a large spoon to scoop out
the avocado cubes.*

Endive & Pear Salad

This elegant salad is also extremely easy to make. Endive looks like tiny little hearts of lettuce. It has a slight bitterness which pairs well with the sweet pear, and the almonds add crunch. While you can cut the endive into half inch pieces, I enjoy leaving the endive leaves whole for a beautiful presentation. Just be sure to serve with a knife as well as a fork so that people can cut the leaves as they eat. Treat endive with gentle care as it's very delicate.

* * * SERVES 4 SIDE SALADS * * *

8 Belgian endives
2 pears, sliced thinly
1/2 cup of blanched and slivered almonds
1/2 to 3/4 cup of Simple Balsamic Vinaigrette,
   p. 118

1. In a small saucepan, toast the almonds over medium-high heat, stirring to cook evenly, as needed. When the nuts are slightly browned, remove from heat and cool on a plate.

2. Endive doesn't have to be washed, unless it especially needs it. Wipe clean with a clean cloth, if needed. Pull off any damaged outer leaves. Cut off the very end of the endive and layer the whole leaves with the sliced pear on a platter or on individual plates. Sprinkle with the toasted almonds. Drizzle with the Simple Balsamic Vinaigrette. Serve.

I used to avoid endive because the price per pound seemed so expensive. But when compared to many bagged lettuce packages, the price per pound is actually cheaper. It turns out that endive wasn't as expensive as I thought, though still a special treat.

Endive is part of the chicory family and is grown using a two step process, which is what gives it that unique pale color.

Chicory stays good longer than many other lettuces, lasting up to 10-14 days in the refrigerator. Keep wrapped in a damp paper towel in an air tight container.

Watercress, Avocado, & Grapefruit Salad

Watercress is both peppery and spicy. The vibrant taste of the grapefruit pairs well with it. Add the shrimp for a light, main dish salad. The shredded apple is the secret to the dressing, a trick I learned from a recipe from a hotel chef published in an old Gourmet magazine. I wasn't sure that I liked watercress, but this version won me over.

* * * SERVES 2-4 MAIN DISH SALADS, 4-6 SIDE SALADS * * *

I large bunch of watercress, washed well and dried, use thin stems and leaves only.

2 small or I large avocado(s)

I large grapefruit

I/2 pound of wild Oregon or Washington caught, cooked small baby shrimp, optional

Dressing:

2 tablespoons of naturally fermented soy sauce or tamari

I/4 cup of raw apple cider vinegar

3 tablespoons extra virgin olive oil

I/2 cup of grated apple (grated with peel on a medium or small grater)

1. Combine all of the ingredients for the dressing in a small jar with a lid and shake to combine, or place in a small bowl and whisk to combine.

2. Slice the avocado. (Cut in half lengthwise and twist. Remove the seed. Slice right in the peel and use a spoon to remove.) Cut off both ends of the grapefruit and set cut side down on a cutting board. Cut down the sides of the grapefruit to remove the peel and most of the pith on the grapefruit. Slice.

3. In a large serving bowl, combine the watercress with the avocado, grapefruit, and the optional shrimp. Toss with the dressing and serve.

Arugula, Grape, & Chicken Salad

This is one of the salads I find myself making over and over again. It's well balanced and fast to make, too. The bite of the arugula pairs very well with the sweet grapes and the mild chicken. The onion and nuts are optional. They round out the salad well, but I often keep it simple with just the grapes, chicken and arugula. I could also easily imagine this with a salty, crumbly cheese, like blue cheese.

* * * SERVES 4 MAIN DISH SALADS * * *

I large bunch of arugula, or 5 ounces of baby arugula

1/2 sweet onion, or red onion, thinly sliced or 2 shallots, minced, optional

I cup of walnuts, or slivered and blanched almonds, optional

I recipe of Roasted Chicken Breast or Sautéed Chicken, pp. 106-108

I cup of grapes, halved (measured after they are cut)

About 3/4 cup of Simple Balsamic Vinaigrette, p. 118

Alternative Dressings:
Sweet Apple Cider Vinaigrette, p. 121
Sweet Onion Poppyseed Dressing, p. 122

1. If using mature arugula, wash thoroughly several times in a bowl of water, until the water runs clean. Dry and place in a large bowl.

2. If using the nuts, toast in a dry pan over medium high heat until browned and fragrant, stirring as needed to prevent burning and promote even browning. Remove from heat and cool.

3. Combine everything except the dressing in a serving bowl, then toss with the Simple Balsamic Vinaigrette.

Holiday Salad: Candied Nuts, Pears & Blue Cheese

This salad is based off of a Nordstrom café recipe (along with the Sweet Apple Cider Vinaigrette). It's been featured at many a family holiday on both sides of our family. Making the candied nuts adds an extra step, but they're so delicious that it's worth it. As I only eat dairy once in a while, I sometimes leave out the blue cheese or replace with chicken for a main dish salad. I especially like this salad with a nice baby lettuce mix.

* * * Serves 4-6 Main dish Salads, 8-10 Side Salads * * *

I batch of Cinnamon Vanilla Candied Nuts, using walnuts, p. 113

I head of lettuce (green or red leaf, romaine, or butterleaf) washed, dried and torn/cut into bite sized pieces, or about 10 cups of baby lettuce mix

2 ripe Bosch or Anjou pears, cored and cut into bite sized pieces

I red bell pepper, seeded and thinly sliced or diced

2 cups (1/2 a pound) blue cheese, crumbled

3/4 to I cup of Sweet Apple Cider Vinaigrette, p. 121

1. Make the candied nuts and cool to room temperature.

2. Combine the lettuce, nuts, pears, cheese, and red bell pepper in a large bowl.

3. Toss with dressing and serve.

Cheese made from pastured cow's milk is always superior to feedlot fed dairy. For example, pastured cheese has four times the amount of CLA, a fat and cancer fighting acid.

Look for local small dairys or for French made cheese (which is much more likely to be grass-fed).

✳ Strawberry & Goat Cheese Salad

When strawberries are bursting with flavor in the height of their season, it is the perfect time to make this delicious salad. You will need two pints of fresh strawberries; one for the dressing and one for the salad. The salty cheese helps balance out the sweetness of the berries and dressing.

*** SERVES 6-8 SIDE SALADS ***

1 pint of strawberries, stemmed and thinly sliced
1 cup of sliced or slivered and blanched almonds
1/2 pound young spinach or salad mix, washed and dried
1/4 to 1/3 pound goat cheese crumbles
About 3/4 cup of Strawberry Vinaigrette, p. 121

1. In a medium size saucepan, toast the almonds over medium high heat, stirring as needed to promote even toasting and prevent burning. Toast until just browned and fragrant. Remove from heat and cool on a plate.

2. Place the spinach or salad mix in a large bowl. Add the strawberries, goat cheese crumbles, and almonds. Toss with the Strawberry Vinaigrette and serve.

Alternative Dressing:
Sweet Onion Poppyseed Dressing, p. 122

Strawberries, like many other berries, are some of the best fruit to eat, in my opinion. Not only are they sublime in flavor, but they are full of antioxidants and other cancer fighting properties.

For example, ellagic acid found in strawberries, raspberries, and blackberries has been shown in the lab to inhibit the growth of tumors caused by certain carcinogens.

Summertime Peach & Chicken Salad

In this salad, the sweet dressing pairs well with the peaches and chicken. This is a very refreshing salad and perfect for the summer. Make sure you read the sidebar for ideas on how to adapt this salad so you can eat it year round!

* * * Serves 4-6 Main Dish Salads or 8-10 Side Salads * * *

1 head of green or red leaf lettuce, washed, dried and cut/torn into bite sized pieces (8-12 cups)
1/2 sweet onion, thinly sliced
4 small or 2 extra large peaches, sliced or cubed
1 recipe of Roasted Chicken or Sautéed Chicken, pp. 106-108, optional for side salad
1 cup of walnuts, or blanched slivered almonds
About 3/4 cup of Sweet Onion Poppyseed Dressing, p. 122

1. Make the salad dressing and the chicken. Set aside.

2. In a dry pan over medium high heat, toast the walnuts or almonds until browned and fragrant, stirring as needed for even browning, and to prevent burning. Remove to a plate to cool.

3. In a large serving bowl combine the lettuce with the peaches, walnuts, onions, and chicken. Toss with the dressing and serve.

Alternative Dressing:
Simple Balsamic Vinaigrette, p. 118
Strawberry Vinaigrette, p. 121
Sweet Apple Cider Vinaigrette, 121

Conventional peaches are unfortunately highly sprayed with pesticides. For that reason, I do recommend buying organic.

I love the juicy peaches in this recipe, but you certainly aren't limited to using them. My recipe testers recommended a wide variety of fruit, such as cubed melon, strawberries, raspberries, or soft pears. Take your pick and adapt at will. If you change the salad according to what's in season, it can be used almost year round.

Grain, Potato, & Legume Salads

Lemony Chickpea Salad

Summer Quinoa Salad

Mexican Quinoa Salad

Tuscan Clam & Bread Salad

Everyday Rice Salad

Tangy Otsu Noodle Salad

French Potato & Asparagus Salad

Tomato Feta Lentil Salad

Cucumber Pepper Lentil Salad

Thai Salad with Noodles

Many of these salads are perfect for picnics and hearty sides (and don't forget the All American Potato Salad in the "Classic Salads" section). They are also great for packing in lunches. Perhaps you could make a double batch: half to serve with a dinner and half to pack in lunches.

When making grain, legume, or potato salads, it's important to layer your flavors so that they don't end up bland. For this reason, I love herbs, both dried and fresh, and the crisp texture of fresh vegetables. Salty cheeses and juicy tomatoes are also delicious in many recipes.

And don't be surprised by the amount of salt that potatoes, legumes and grains soak up. They are thirsty for salt and won't be satisfied until you've salted them well. Too often, a bland salad is simply a case of being under-salted. So when I say, "Salt to taste," I truly mean it. Freshly ground pepper is another simple way to enhance the flavors already present.

I also soak my legumes and grains overnight as detailed in the following recipes. This is a topic I've discussed on my blog (thenourishinggourmet. com). While the topic is too large to fully address in this book, soaking grains and legumes may not only decrease anti-nutrients that block you from absorbing nutrients, but also make them more digestible. Truthfully, I believe that the texture improves dramatically. My soaked brown rice, for example, has a much lighter, fluffier texture and is better received by those accustomed to white rice. However, if you would rather not soak your grains overnight, just make according to the typical instructions and proceed with the recipe.

✳ Lemony Chickpea Salad

I love the bright flavor the lemon zest adds to this salad. This recipe is easily adaptable. Mix it up by using white beans, or trying different fresh herbs (such as basil) instead of the parsley. I like to serve this right after it's dressed. However, if you have some leftovers, simply re-season with lemon juice and salt and pepper before serving. Because chickpeas are higher in omega 6 fatty acids, adding omega 3 rich salmon or low mercury tuna gives not only a great taste profile, but balances out the omega fatty acids.

* * * Serves 6 small servings * * *

3 cups of cooked chickpeas, canned or homemade,
   p. 115 *or white beans*
1/2 red onion, finely chopped
1 large stick of celery, diced
About 20 stems of parsley, stemmed and chopped

Dressing:
1 teaspoon lemon zest
1/4 cup of fresh lemon juice
1/4 cup of olive oil
1 teaspoon unrefined salt
1 garlic clove, peeled and finely minced or put
   through a garlic press
Freshly ground pepper

1. In a medium sized bowl, combine the salad ingredients.

2. Make the salad dressing and pour over the chickpea salad. Gently stir to combine. Taste test and adjust flavors, if needed, with more salt and freshly ground pepper, lemon juice or oil.

Variation with Salmon or Tuna: Add about 1 to 1 1/2 cups of canned or slow roasted salmon, p. 114, or Wild Planet's canned tuna.

I keep a few cans of Eden's canned beans in my cupboard for last minute meals. They are canned in BPA free cans and are salt free (so I can add my own unrefined salt) and cooked with kombu, a seaweed that adds minerals, taste, and helps make the beans more digestible.

However, having your own homemade frozen beans is so much more affordable. I try to cook my own beans most of the time, and it makes dishes like this a very frugal one to make.

Summer Quinoa Salad

Flavorful quinoa is mixed with summer vegetables, dressed with a lemon pepper dressing, and topped with fresh herbs. This salad can be served warm, room temperature, or my favorite version, chilled. This is a perfect salad to make the day before a picnic outing, as it does well with 24 hours in the refrigerator.

* * * Serves 8-10 Side Servings * * *

2 cups of quinoa
2 tablespoons raw apple cider vinegar
1 teaspoon unrefined salt
4 small zucchini, stemmed and cubed
1 large red pepper, seeded and cubed
2 tablespoons of coconut oil, olive oil, Mary's Oil Blend, p. 110, or a combination of butter and olive oil
4 ears of corn (or about 2 cups of frozen corn)
1/2 bunch of Italian flat leaf parsley
8-10 large basil leaves
Lemon Pepper Dressing, p. 119 (with garlic, if desired)
Salt and Pepper

1. The night before, place the quinoa in a medium sized bowl with 2 cups of warm water and the apple cider vinegar. Cover and leave in a warm room for 12-24 hours to reduce anti-nutrients.

2. In a small strainer, drain the quinoa, then rinse thoroughly. Put in a medium sized pot with 2 cups of fresh water and 1 teaspoon unrefined salt. Bring to a boil, covered, then reduce heat and cook for 12 minutes. Turn cooked quinoa into a large bowl or jellyroll pan to cool.

3. Meanwhile, cut the corn off the cob (stand upright and run a knife down the sides of the cob). Heat the oil in a large saucepan over medium-high heat until hot and add the zucchini and red pepper. Sprinkle with a bit of salt and sauté, stirring as needed, until the vegetables are just tender. Add the corn in the last minute or two. Add to the quinoa to cool.

4. Once the quinoa and vegetables are no longer hot, dress with the lemon pepper dressing and toss in the herbs. Serve room temperature, warm, or chilled. Adjust with salt and pepper if needed.

I use a method of soaking grains that helpes reduce anti-nutrients in them and makes them more easily digested.

Once I switched over to this method, I found that my tummy didn't feel so heavy after eating grains, and the grains themselves seemed lighter, with a better texture. All in all, a win-win solution. It's a simple practice, just takes some forethought.

Mexican Quinoa Salad

I love this salad. It's based off of a salad I enjoyed at my local New Seasons Market store. As soon as I tried it, I knew I had to create my own version. It's remained a favorite ever since. Once again, I've included directions for soaking the quinoa overnight for better texture, taste and nutrition.

* * * SERVES 8-10 SIDE SALADS * * *

2 cups of quinoa
2 cups of warm water
2 tablespoons raw apple cider vinegar
1 teaspoon salt
1 bunch of spinach
1 large red bell pepper, cored and diced
2 cobs of corn, corn cut off the cob, or 2 cups of
    frozen corn
2 tablespoons butter
1/2 large bunch of cilantro, or 1 small bunch of
    cilantro, washed, stemmed and roughly chopped

Dressing:
3/4 cup of mild olive oil
1/4 cup of raw apple cider vinegar
1 teaspoon ground cumin
1/4 teaspoon cayenne pepper
1 teaspoon unrefined salt
1/2 teaspoon dried oregano
3 garlic cloves, peeled and finely minced or put
    through a garlic press

1. Combine the two cups of warm water, quinoa and raw apple cider vinegar in a large bowl. Cover and put in a warm place for 12-24 hours. Drain and rinse well in a fine sieve. Place the quinoa in a medium size pot with 2 cups of fresh water and 1 teaspoon of unrefined salt. Bring to a boil, then lower heat and cook, covered on low heat for 12 minutes. Place in a large bowl or spread over a jellyroll pan to cool.

2. Wash the spinach well and cut off the stems. In a large covered saucepan add the spinach and 1/3 cup of water. Cook over medium-high heat until the spinach is wilted. Drain in sieve and let cool. Squeeze all extra moisture out of the spinach and then roughly chop.

3. Melt the butter in the same large saucepan over medium-high heat and add the corn. Cook, stirring as needed, until the corn is just cooked through (about 2 minutes).

4. Make the dressing by combining all of the dressing ingredients in a jar and shaking vigorously to combine. Combine the cooled quinoa, spinach, corn, red bell peppers, and cilantro. Toss with the dressing (saving about 1/4 cup of it). Serve right away, or refrigerate. If refrigerated, toss with the rest of the dressing right before serving.

Tuscan Clam & Bread Salad

Pan-fried croutons with juicy sweet tomatoes, fresh basil, and sweet manila clams are dressed with the lemon pepper dressing for a delightful twist on Panzanella (Tuscan Bread Salad). Make sure that you use really good tomatoes in this recipe.

* * * SERVES 4 MAIN DISH SERVINGS, 8 SIDE SERVINGS * * *

6 pieces of bread (sourdough whole wheat, sprouted whole wheat or spelt, or a gluten free variety), cubed

3 garlic cloves, peeled and smashed, but left whole

2 tablespoons each of olive oil and butter, or 1/4 cup of coconut oil or Mary's Oil Blend, p. 110

Unrefined Salt

8 ounces of cherry or grape tomatoes washed and cut in half (never refrigerate tomatoes- it ruins their texture)

Large handful of fresh basil

1 pound of fresh manila clams (on the small side)

1/2 cup of white wine plus 1/4 cup of water, or 3/4 cup of water

About 1/2 cup of Lemon Pepper Dressing with Garlic, p. 119

1. Make the Croutons: In two batches, fry the croutons in a large pan over medium high heat with the garlic and fat of choice. Stir to brown evenly. When croutons are browned and crunchy, remove to a serving bowl and repeat. Use more fat if needed for the second batch and fish out the garlic from the first batch to reuse. Remove garlic from the croutons, and sprinkle with salt when finished.

2. Roll the basil leaves up into a single "cigar" and cut into thin shreds. Add the basil and the halved small tomatoes to the croutons.

3. Drain the manila clams and discard any that are cracked or won't close when gently pressed together. In a large saucepan with a lid (I use the same one I made the croutons in), bring 3/4 cup of water or the wine/water mixture to a boil. Add the clams and cook until all of them are open (about 3-5 minutes for small clams). If any don't open, discard. Remove from shells with a slotted spoon to a plate and let cool several minutes.

4. Add the clams to the other ingredients and toss with the lemon pepper dressing. Serve right away.

To care for manila clams, make sure that they always have air so they don't suffocate. When you bring them home, scrub them well and throw away any cracked clams, or any open ones that won't close when gently pressed together. Place in a bowl of cool water with a couple of tablespoons of salt (this helps them purge any salt they have), and leave in the refrigerator for a couple of hours before using.

Everyday Rice Salad

I love this salad. It's refreshing, can be made year round, and is so frugal. This has long been a staple at our house. You can easily vary the ingredients in the salad, and to plump it up more with protein, add leftover chopped up meat to the mix.

* * * SERVES 4-6 MAIN DISH SALADS OR 8-10 SIDE SALADS * * *

2 cups of brown basmati rice
2 tablespoons raw apple cider vinegar
1 teaspoon unrefined salt
2-3 medium carrots, shredded
2 celery sticks, finely sliced or diced
2 tablespoons butter
1 cup of frozen peas
4 eggs, cracked and gently whisked in a small bowl
3/4 to 1 cup of Everyday Salad Dressing, p. 118

1. In a non reactive bowl (such as glass or ceramic) place the rice and apple cider vinegar and 2 cups of warm water. Cover and leave in a warm place for 12-24 hours.

2. Drain in a fine sieve placed over a 4 cup glass measuring cup or a small bowl (note exactly how much water is drained). Rinse the rice and place in a medium pot. Add the *same amount* of fresh water as you drained and *measured from the soaked rice.* Then add 2 cups more of fresh water. Add 1 teaspoon salt. Cover and bring to a boil, lower heat to low and cook for 45 minutes. Turn out into a large bowl or jellyroll pan to cool.

3. In a medium saucepan, melt the butter over medium heat. When the pan and butter are hot, add the peas and cook until cooked through. Add to rice. In the same pan (add more butter if needed), add the whisked eggs and cook, stirring with a wooden spoon or fork until done. Add to rice.

4. Add the carrots and celery and then toss with the dressing. Season with unrefined salt and/or freshly ground pepper as desired. Serve at room temperature, or chilled.

Alternative Dressing:
Lemon Pepper Dressing with Basil and Garlic, p. 119

Tangy Otsu Noodle Salad

This refreshing salad has Asian flavor elements with the soy sauce, toasted sesame oil and ginger. The lemon zest and juice really makes the flavor pop. Buckwheat noodles would be the more traditional noodle to use (which we love), but you can also use brown rice spaghetti style noodles. When made the day before, the flavors soak into the noodles for a slightly different flavor profile. You can add other vegetables, such as thinly sliced cabbage or red pepper, too.

* * * SERVES 4-6 MAIN DISH SALADS OR 8-10 SIDE SALADS * * *

1 pound of buckwheat or brown rice spaghetti style noodles

Dressing Ingredients:
Grated zest of one lemon
2 tablespoons each of lemon juice and raw apple cider vinegar
1 tablespoon grated ginger
3 garlic cloves, peeled and finely minced or put through a garlic press
1/4 to 1/2 teaspoon cayenne pepper (vary to how much heat you want)
1 tablespoon honey, preferably raw
4 tablespoons toasted sesame oil
1/2 cup of naturally fermented soy sauce or tamari (gluten free)

Salad Ingredients:
2 tablespoons raw sesame seeds, hulled
1 head of cilantro, washed, stemmed and minced
2 carrots, peeled and grated on a medium sized grater
1 cucumber, peeled, seeded, and cut into thin two inch strips

1. Cook the noodles in salted water according to the directions on the package. Drain and rinse with cold water.

2. Combine the dressing ingredients in a Mason jar or a small bowl. Whisk or shake before tossing.

3. Toast the sesame seeds in a dry pan, stirring to brown evenly, over medium high heat. Remove from heat.

4. In a large serving bowl, combine the noodles with the vegetables, sesame seeds, and optional main dish ingredients. Toss with the dressing and serve at room temperature. Can be made the day before.

Stays good up to 3 days.

Main Dish Version: Add 1 recipe of Roasted Chicken Breast, p. 106, Sautéed Chicken, p. 108, Juicy Grassfed Steak, p. 104, or Slow Roasted Salmon, p. 114.

✳ French Potato & Asparagus Salad

This simple salad has been a favorite when I've shared it with others. Instead of a mayonnaise based dressing, this potato salad is dressed with a vinaigrette, for an equally delicious salad. I love this salad both warm and cold, though my husband much prefers it cold. Don't serve hot.

* * * 8-10 Side Servings * * *

3 pounds of <u>red</u> or Yukon gold potatoes, peeled if
   desired (see p. 23)
I pound of asparagus
1/4 cup of apple cider vinegar
10-12 fresh basil leaves, rolled into a single 'cigar'
   and thinly sliced
About 3/4 cup of Everyday Salad Dressing, p. 118

1. Cube the potatoes into I to 1/2 inch pieces. Place in a large pot and just cover with water. Add 2 tablespoons of unrefined salt. Bring to a boil over high heat. Lower heat and simmer for around 7 minutes, or until the potatoes are just tender.

2. Meanwhile, cut off the woody stems of the asparagus and cut into 2 inch pieces. Bring I inch of water to a boil in a medium pot, with a steam basket, if you have one.
Add the asparagus and steam for 3-4 minutes, or until the asparagus is just tender. To prevent them from cooking any longer, shock in a bowl of cold water (optional).

3. Drain the potatoes and asparagus in a large colander. Sprinkle with apple cider vinegar and let cool.

4. Once the potatoes are cool, dress with everyday salad dressing and the basil. Salt and Pepper to taste.

> *You can easily take the basic concept of this dish and play around with the ingredients. My only caution would be to keep it simple, as that's part of the beauty of the dish. Green beans in place of the asparagus, chopped boiled eggs, or adding in chicken or white beans to make it a main dish salad are some of the ideas I've had.*

✕ Two French Lentil Salads

*French lentils hold their shape better than brown lentils, so they work well in
cold salads. They also have a lovely peppery flavor. You can substitute brown or beluga lentils.
The soaking makes the lentils more digestible and helps them cook faster. The optional
kombu adds minerals to the dish as well as helping make the beans more digestible.*

* * * 4-6 SIDE SERVINGS * * *

Tomato & Feta Lentil Salad

1 cup of French green lentils
1 strip of kombu (a seaweed), optional
1/4 pound of feta, crumbled or cut into
  bite-sized pieces
4 ounces of baby tomatoes, cut in half
Handful of herbs such as basil or parsley
1/3 to 1/2 cup of Simple Balsamic Vinaigrette,
  p. 118

1. Soak the lentils in plenty of warm water for 8-24
hours. Drain and rinse. Place the lentils in a medium pot
and cover with plenty of fresh water. Place one kombu
strip in the water, if using. Bring to a low simmer and
cook until the lentils are tender, but still holding their
shape; 30-60 minutes, depending on how old the lentils
are. Drain, remove kombu strip and let cool.

2. Add the tomatoes and feta and dress with the balsamic
vinaigrette. Top with fresh herbs. Salt, if needed. Serve
right away or refrigerate to serve later. The flavors will
meld as it sits.

Cucumber & Pepper Lentil salad

1 cup of French green lentils
1 cucumber, peeled and diced
6-8 multicolored mini sweet peppers (or 2 large
  peppers), stemmed, seeded and diced
Handful of herbs such as basil or parsley
1/3 to 1/2 cup of Simple Balsamic Vinaigrette,
  p. 118

1. Soak the lentils in plenty of warm water for 8-24
hours. Drain and rinse. Place the lentils in a medium pot
and cover with plenty of fresh water. Place one kombu
strip in the water, if using. Bring to a low simmer and
cook until the lentils are tender, but still holding their
shape; 30-60 minutes, depending on how old the lentils
are. Drain, remove kombu strip and let cool.

2. Add the cucumber, sweet peppers, and herbs to the
lentils. Toss with the balsamic vinaigrette. Salt well (I find
that this salad soaks up salt and needs more than you
would think).

Thai Noodle Salad

This refreshing salad is a mixed lettuce and noodle salad, making it light and refreshing, but filling as well. The herbs are important as they add a lovely fragrant component to the dish. Make it a main dish by adding chicken or beef.

* * * 4-6 Main Dish Servings or 8-10 Side Servings * * *

1 small head of romaine lettuce, or half a large head

2 medium sized carrots, peeled and cut into matchsticks

2 cucumbers, peeled if desired, seeded and cut into matchsticks

1 red bell pepper, seeded, stemmed and thinly sliced

1 small bunch of cilantro, washed and stemmed

Handful of fresh basil, washed (Thai basil if available)

Handful of fresh mint, washed, optional

8 ounces brown rice spaghetti noodles, or noodles of choice

Dressing Ingredients:

1/4 cup of fresh lime juice

1 to 1 1/2 teaspoon lime zest

3/4 cup of mild olive oil, sesame oil (or a mixture of the two), or Mary's Oil Blend, p. 110

4 tablespoons soy sauce or tamari (gluten free)

2 tablespoons of honey, preferably raw

1/4 to 1/2 teaspoon cayenne pepper

1 tablespoon grated fresh ginger

1-3 garlic cloves, peeled and put through a garlic press

1. Cook the noodles according to the package directions. Rinse with cold water to cool, and then coat with a bit of oil to prevent sticking. Place in a large bowl.

2. While the noodles are cooking, place all of the dressing ingredients into a lidded jar. If the honey is solid, melt in a saucepan over low heat until just liquefied.

3. Using a sharp knife, slice the lettuce into 1/2 inch shreds, then wash and dry. Add with the vegetables and herbs to a bowl of noodles. If the basil or mint leaves are large, tear into smaller pieces or mince with a knife.

4. Give the dressing a vigorous shake and toss with the salad ingredients. Serve.

Other Additions:

Sliced Juicy Grassfed Steak, p. 104

Roasted Chicken, p. 106

Vegetable Side Salads

Simple Green Bean Salad

Simple Carrot Salad

Simple Roasted Beet & Orange Salad

Cucumber & Red Onion Salad

Fennel & Bacon Salad

Lemon Garlic Mushroom Salad

Zucchini Carpaccio with Pinenuts & Basil

I believe that food should be simple. If it's overly complicated, homemade food will be relegated to lazy Saturdays and entertaining. But I also don't think that food should be overly simple. Too often, vegetables are overcooked and served without any adorning, an unappetizing combination.

For this section, I've tried to keep the recipes simple, so they can be made often. I've also tried to adorn them with flavor so that the vegetables are appetizing and enjoyable. Many of the following recipes are my family's favorites, and can be made in minutes, such as the Simple Carrot Salad and the Cucumber and Red Onion Salad. The Simple Carrot Salad has been a staple in my family for years and my four-year-old daughter has grown up enjoying it.

I've also included some recipes that are more in the "gourmet" category, like the Fennel and Bacon Salad and the Lemon Garlic Mushroom Salad. I find it fun to try new flavors and experiment with fresh ideas. I hope that you enjoy all of the recipes.

Simple Green Bean Salad

Steamed green beans are shocked in cold water and dressed with a favorite vinaigrette.
The toasted walnuts and onions are optional, but really add a lot of texture and flavor.
Although simple, this is a delicious side salad. One suggestion to try (from one of
my recipe testers) is to replace the green beans in this recipe with broccoli.

* * * 4 SERVINGS * * *

1 pound of green beans, washed and trimmed
   (trim just the stem end and keep the beans long
   for a pretty presentation)
1/3 to 1/2 cup of dressing of choice (Creamy
   Roasted Garlic Dressing or Double Garlic
   Dressing, p. 120, or Simple Balsamic
   Vinaigrette, p. 118)
1/2 cup of walnuts, optional
1/2 cup of finely chopped red onion (about one
   half of a medium sized red onion), optional

1. Heat 1/2 to 1 inch of water in a covered medium pot on
high heat (using a steamer basket if you have one). Once
boiling, add the green beans and steam on low heat for 5-7
minutes or until the green beans are just crisp tender. Remove
the green beans to a bowl full of ice-cold water to shock
the beans and prevent them from cooking longer. Pat beans
dry and place in serving bowl.

2. Toast the walnuts in a dry pan over medium high heat,
stirring to evenly brown, until fragrant and lightly browned.
Remove to a cutting board and finely chop. Add to the green
beans with the chopped red onion and toss with your choice
of dressing. Salt and pepper if needed. Serve at room temperature. Can be made the day before. Keep in the refrigerator.

Sometimes the best way to treat a veg-
etable is to buy it as fresh as possible,
use it soon, and cook it simply. You
want to enhance the natural flavors of
the vegetable, not mask it.

In this recipe, I love the crunch of the
nuts and raw onion in contrast to the
cooked green beans.

✳ Simple Carrot Salad

A family favorite, this salad pairs sweet carrots with more savory ingredients, such as garlic and mustard. It's delicious and simple enough to make often. You can add chopped and toasted nuts, such as walnuts or almonds for extra crunch, if desired. For a long time, this salad was featured on my menu once a week.

* * * 4-6 SERVINGS * * *

6 medium carrots peeled and shredded (a food processor makes this job fast), about 4 cups of carrot shreds

1 tablespoon balsamic vinegar

1 tablespoon raw apple cider vinegar

1 teaspoon brown mustard (Eden's Organic Brown Mustard or Dijon style mustard)

2 tablespoons extra virgin olive oil

1 garlic clove, peeled and finely minced or put through a garlic press.

1/2 teaspoon dried basil, or about 1 tablespoon minced fresh basil

1/2 teaspoon unrefined salt and freshly ground pepper

Carrots are amazing. They have a high amount of carotenoids. Some research suggests that high carotenoid consumption can lead to a decrease in bladder, cervix, prostate, colon, larynx, esophageal, and some breast cancers. Some of the nutrients in carrots are fat-soluble. That means it is good that this recipe contains some fat as you can better absorb those nutrients with it.

Put shredded carrots in a bowl, mix the rest of the ingredients in a small bowl and pour over carrots. Gently toss. Taste and adjust with salt, pepper and extra vinegar and oil, if needed.

You can serve right away, or chill before serving. The carrots will lose some of their crunch if marinated too long.

Simple Roasted Beet & Orange Salad

Roasting brings out the natural sweetness of beets while the acidic and sweet orange pairs wonderfully for a classic combination. The dressing is simple: the juice gathered while preparing the oranges with olive oil and salt and pepper. So simple but so good. Tip: I often roast garlic at the same time as the beets so that I can make my Roasted Garlic Dressing!

* * * 4-6 SERVINGS * * *

4 medium beets
Butter, Mary's Oil Blend, p.110, or olive oil
4 medium/small oranges
Olive oil
Unrefined salt and freshly ground pepper

Preheat oven to 400 degrees Fahrenheit

1. Wash beets, dry and rub with butter or oil. Poke with a fork a couple of times and place in a pie pan. Cook for 1 to 1 1/2 hours, or until a thin sharp knife easily pierces the middle of the largest beet. Cool.

2. Peel the cooled beets with a small sharp knife and cut into thin slices. Peel the oranges with a small sharp knife by cutting off the ends of the orange and then holding the orange on the cutting board, cutting down the sides of the orange to remove the rest of the peel. Thinly slice and remove any seeds. Any juice that accumulates on the cutting board should be poured over the beets.

3. To serve, overlap the orange and beets in an alternating pattern on a platter. If any orange was cut off with the peel, squeeze over the salad, then drizzle with a bit of olive oil (about 1 to 2 tablspoons). Sprinkle unrefined salt over the salad and serve.

Beets are traditionally considered a good liver cleanser. They are a source of betaine and folate, which work in a synergy to reduce homocysteine, an amino acid that can be harmful to blood vessels. They also contain a high amount of potassium.

Cucumber & Red Onion Salad

This favorite salad takes just a few minutes to throw together and is one of our favorites, especially in the summer. It's very refreshing and light. It serves 4 small side servings, but I could eat the whole bowl myself! I cut the cucumbers chunky on the diagonal, so that they remain crunchy, even when left in the refrigerator for a day or two.

* * * 4 SERVINGS * * *

2 medium sized cucumbers
1/2 medium red onion, peeled and thinly sliced
2 tablespoons extra virgin olive oil
2 tablespoons raw apple cider vinegar
3/4 teaspoon celery seed
3/4 teaspoon unrefined salt
2 to 3 garlic cloves, peeled and finely minced or
   put through a garlic press

1. Peel the cucumbers, cut off the stems, and cut in half lengthwise. Seed by running a spoon down the middle of the cucumber. Cut each half in half again lengthwise, and then slice into 1/2 inch thick pieces on a diagonal. Place in a serving bowl with the thinly sliced onion.

2. Measure the rest of the ingredients right into the bowl and toss. Serve right away, or refrigerate until you serve. Toss again right before serving. Will keep up to 2 days.

Why are cucumbers supposed to be good for your skin? They are a source of silica, an essential component to connective tissue. They are also perfectly cooling on a hot day, which is why I love this salad during the summer. Bring it along on a picnic or serve as a side to a barbecue.

Fennel & Bacon Salad

Fresh fennel bulb has a light licorice flavor and a crunchy texture when eaten raw. The secret to a raw fennel salad is slicing the fennel very thinly. This salad was inspired by a dish I was served at a small local restaurant. They used smoked pig cheek, but I found that my home version with bacon is just as good.

* * * 4 SERVINGS * * *

1 pound of fennel bulb (about 1 large, or two
    smallish bulbs)
4 thick cut nitrate free bacon slices
1/3 to 1/2 cup Lemon Pepper Dressing with Garlic,
    p. 119

1. In a large saucepan fry the bacon on medium heat (nitrate free bacon burns a little more easily, so it does better at a lower temperature). Flip frequently until both sides are well browned. Remove to a plate to cool, then crumble into bite size pieces.

2. Cut off the fronds, if any, of the fennel. Slice just a thin slice off the bottom of the fennel as well. If you are using a large fennel bulb, you will need to peel the tough outer layer off with a vegetable peeler. Cut in half, then place cut side down on a cutting board. Slice as thinly as possible with a sharp knife. Toss right away with the Lemon Pepper Dressing to prevent browning. Sprinkle with the bacon pieces or mix in, as desired for presentation. Serve right away. Decorate with a few pieces of the fennel frond if you have any.

Fennel has been cultivated since ancient times. It has antioxidant value, as well as being a good source of vitamin C. The seed of the fennel is used to calm the muscles in the stomach. For that reason, it's been used in research on infant colic with promising results.

✳ Lemon Garlic Mushroom Salad

I thought I wasn't a fan of either raw mushrooms or zucchini, but I actually love both of these salads. The mushroom salad is great year round. The lemony dressing brightens a winter or summer day alike.

* * * 4 SERVINGS * * *

1 pound of mushrooms, white or crimini
1/4 cup of chopped parsley
About 1/2 cup of Lemon Pepper Dressing with Garlic, p. 119

Gently wash the mushrooms with a damp washcloth. Cut a small sliver off the end of each stem, then thinly slice the mushrooms with a sharp knife. Place in a bowl and toss with the lemon pepper garlic dressing and the parsley. Serve. Since mushrooms act like a sponge, they will continue to soak up the dressing. Re-toss any leftovers with more dressing.

What you see labeled as white and crimini mushrooms in the supermarket are actually the same variety of mushroom, so buy whichever one you prefer. While there are certainly some more expensive superstar mushrooms, even the common mushroom is a good source of many nutrients.

What about zucchini? Zucchini is a good source of natural sodium, which your adrenals love. It is also a great source of potassium.

✳ Zucchini Carpaccio with Pinenuts and Basil

Zucchini carpaccio is a perfect summer salad. It's so refreshing, and when the raw zucchini is thinly sliced it has a great texture. It also makes a lovely presentation. You can replace the pinenuts with slivered and blanched almonds, if desired.

* * * 4 SERVINGS * * *

2 medium zucchini
2 tablespoons fresh lemon juice
1 tablespoon olive oil
About 1/2 teaspoon unrefined salt
Handful of basil, washed
2-4 tablespoons pinenuts

1. In a small dry saucepan, toast the pinenuts over medium-high heat until they are starting to brown. Stir as needed to cook evenly and prevent burning.

2. Cut off the ends of the zucchini, and using a very sharp knife, slice very thinly. Roll all of the basil leaves into a single "cigar" and slice thinly. Place the zucchini and basil in a bowl and sprinkle with the lemon juice, olive oil, and salt. Toss to coat. Sprinkle the pinenuts over the top and serve.

Lettuce Wraps

Apple Cranberry Turkey Salad

Soy & Sesame Chicken Wraps

Taco Wraps

Moroccan Beef or Lamb Wraps

Vietnamese Lettuce Wraps with Two Dips

Chicken and Peach Wraps

Everyday Lettuce Wraps

Who doesn't love playing with their food? Lettuce wraps are a fun way to eat your salad. I find them popular both with children and meat lovers, as the protein based filling is the focus of the meal. Calling them lettuce wraps is a little deceptive, as most of the time you aren't actually wrapping the lettuce into a roll, but rather using it as a "bowl" or "cup" for the filling. But regardless, they are tasty!

You can turn many of the main dish green salads into salad fillings, like I did with the Chicken and Peach green salad. All you need to do is put all of the ingredients (other than the lettuce) in a bowl, dress with the appropriate salad dressing, and serve with lettuce to wrap.

Which brings me to the question of what kind of lettuce to use for salad wraps. Popular restaurant recipes for salad wraps use iceberg lettuce, for the crunch and because the shape is a perfect vehicle for filling. However, iceberg isn't my favorite lettuce to use as it's a lightweight nutritionally speaking. So below are some even better choices.

Bibb or Butterleaf Lettuce: Almost sweet, and well, buttery! These gentle leaves form cups when separated at the base, which make them a great choice for lettuce wraps.

Cabbage: Cabbage gives serious crunch to a lettuce wrap and a stronger flavor. We find cabbage leaves a little too thick to enjoy, but I have friends who use these often, particularly when making Taco Wraps.

Radicchio: Crisp and slightly bitter, these little red heads of lettuce from the chicory family form perfect little "bowls" for filling.

Endive (Escarole or Broad Leaved Endive): Also from the chicory family, endive has pale green leaves and a slightly bitter taste. It forms long thin cups that also make a great vehicle for filling.

Romaine or Red or Green Leaf Lettuces: For actual lettuce "wraps", cut the stem out of romaine or leaf lettuce and use the leaves to wrap around filling of choice.

Apple Cranberry Turkey Salad

This gentle salad is bright with fruit flavor from the dried cranberries and diced fresh apple. Perfect for the fall, though appreciated year round, this recipe is a family favorite. While turkey is the best foil for the cranberries, chicken works as well.

* * * 4 SERVINGS * * *

2 cups of leftover roasted turkey or cooked
chicken breast, diced or shredded
1 large green apple, washed and diced *pear*
1 cup of dried cranberries, preferably fruit juice
sweetened *cranberry sauce*
1 cup of walnuts
2 large celery sticks, washed and diced
3/4 cup of mayonnaise, p. 111 (see the resource
section, pp. 124-125, for storebought options)
1 tablespoon brown mustard (Eden's organic
brown mustard or Dijon style mustard)
1 tablespoon raw apple cider vinegar

1. Toast the walnuts in a dry medium sized pan over medium high heat, stirring as needed, until browned and fragrant. Remove from heat and cool. Roughly chop.

2. Combine the turkey, green apple, cranberries, celery and walnuts in a large serving bowl. In a small bowl mix together the mayonnaise, mustard, and vinegar. Toss with the other ingredients. Taste test and adjust if needed with salt, vinegar, pepper, or mustard.

3. Serve over a bed of lettuce (arugula, red leaf, butterleaf, etc), use as a filling for a lettuce wrap, or serve as is.

This is a perfect salad to make with leftover turkey from Thanksgiving. All of the extra fruit and celery fill the dish out and add loads of flavor and crunch. Of course, year round, this is easy to make with leftover roasted chicken, too.

☀ Soy & Sesame Chicken Wraps

This is a great last minute meal as it only takes minutes to make. It's perfect for a busy week night. Soy sauce adds saltiness and depth and the toasted sesame oil adds a dark flavor. The toasted sesame seeds are optional as their flavor is mostly buried by the rich undertones of the toasted sesame oil; they still look very pretty when sprinkled over top.

* * * 2-4 SERVINGS * * *

1 tablespoon coconut oil, butter,
   Mary's Oil Blend, p. 110, or fat of choice
1 pound of ground chicken meat (turkey would
   work as well)
1 tablespoon grated fresh ginger
1 to 3 garlic cloves, peeled and finely minced or
   put through a garlic press
1 tablespoon soy sauce or tamari
1/2 teaspoon toasted sesame oil — *butter*
1 tablespoon sesame seeds — *sunflower*
2-3 green onions, washed
About 1/2 head of butterleaf or bib lettuce, or
   one head of radicchio

1. In a small saucepan, toast the sesame seeds over medium high heat, stirring as needed to prevent burning and promote even browning. Remove from heat and cool on a plate.

2. Carefully separate the individual leaves of lettuce and wash and dry thoroughly, but gently.

3. In a large saucepan, add the fat of choice and the chicken meat, ginger and garlic. Cook, stirring to cook evenly, until the chicken is completely cooked through.

4. Stir in the soy sauce or tamari and toasted sesame oil. Cut off the root ends of the green onion and the top two inches or so of the green part. Thinly slice.

5. To serve, sprinkle the toasted sesame seeds and green onions over the chicken mixture and serve with the lettuce leaves alongside.

Taco Wraps

We love tacos, burritos, and other Mexican inspired foods.
This is a refreshing take on tacos as it uses lettuce as the taco shell.
You can pile in your favorite taco fillings for a delightful meal.

* * * 4 SERVINGS * * *

I medium head of bibb, red or green leaf lettuce,
washed and dried
I recipe of Mexican Ground Beef, p. 105

Toppings (choose which ones you want)
1-2 large avocadoes, peeled and cut into bite sized
pieces
Sliced black olives
Shredded cheddar cheese (preferably grass fed
and raw)
Diced tomatoes
Sour cream
Creamy Mexican Avocado Dressing, p. 122
Salsa
Bunch of cilantro, washed, stemmed and chopped

You can avoid the chemical, ferrous gluconate, that is used to turn green olives black, by buying from companies like the Santa Barbara Olive Company, or buying green olives rather than black. The black olives from Santa Barbara Olive Company have a more grayish appearance compared to their chemically treated counterparts.

Arrange all of the lettuce and toppings on a large platter or in
small bowls. Allow everyone to serve themselves. Layer meat
first, then toppings of choice, and finally add sour cream,
salsa, or Creamy Mexican Avocado Dressing.

*Moroccan Beef or Lamb Wraps

This salad wrap recipe is one of the more filling ones when paired with the tahini sauce. The beef is spiced with both spicy and sweet spices, making it popular with adults and children. I have offered two sauce recipes. Choose one, or make both! You could also garnish with finely minced mint for added flavor.

* * * 4 SERVINGS * * *

I to 1 1/2 pounds of ground beef, preferably 100% grassfed
2 garlic cloves, peeled and finely minced or put through a garlic press
I teaspoon ground turmeric
1/4 to 1/2 teaspoon cayenne powder
1/2 teaspoon ground cinnamon
1/2 teaspoon ground nutmeg
1/2 teaspoon black pepper
1/2 teaspoon ground ginger
Unrefined salt
I cucumber, peeled and thinly sliced
I large tomato, thinly sliced
I head of bibb, butterleaf, red or green leaf lettuce, or radicchio, washed and dried

In a large saucepan, add the beef with all of the spices and garlic. Cook over medium high heat until cooked all the way through, stirring to cook evenly. When using grassfed beef, your beef will be lean and won't need to be drained. If needed, push all of the meat to one side of the pan and tilt the pan to pool the grease on the other side. Spoon the grease out. Salt to taste.

Serve with the cucumbers, tomatoes, lettuce and dip(s) of choice.

Cucumber Yogurt Sauce
I cucumber, peeled, seeded, and thinly sliced.
I teaspoon of unrefined salt
I cup of plain, whole milk yogurt
2-3 garlic cloves, peeled and minced or put through a garlic press

Place the sliced cucumbers in a sieve over a bowl and sprinkle the salt over it. The salt will pull the water out of the cucumber and you will start to see water pool in the bowl. Leave for one hour. You can gently squeeze the cucumber slices to release more water as well at the end of the hour. Mix the cucumbers, garlic, and yogurt in a bowl. Taste and add salt, if needed.

Lemon Tahini Sauce
1/4 cup tahini (ground sesame seeds)
1/4 cup of fresh lemon
I large garlic clove, peeled and finely minced or put through a garlic press
2 tablespoons water
2 tablespoons of extra virgin olive oil
1/2 teaspoon cumin

Stir the tahini paste and lemon juice with a fork until combined. Add the rest of the ingredients and whisk until smooth. Can add more water if needed to thin. Add salt if needed.

Vietnamese Lettuce Wraps with Two Dips

Refreshing, herby, and satisfying, this recipe is well-loved by our family. We enjoy eating at Vietnamese restaurants, but I wanted to create a similar recipe at home that doesn't use a lot of hard to find ingredients. We were quite happy with the results. You can make just one of the dips, if desired, but we definitely like having both. It's nice to dip a bite into each! You can also add thinly sliced red pepper to this recipe.

* * * 4 SERVINGS * * *

1 small head bibb or butterleaf lettuce, leaves separated and washed and dried

2 carrots, peeled and cut into matchsticks

1 large cucumber, seeded, peeled and cut into matchsticks

Large handful of basil, or Thai basil if available

1/2 bunch of cilantro, washed, dried, and stemmed

1 small bunch of fresh mint, washed and dried, optional

1 recipe of Roasted Chicken Breast or Sautéed Chicken, p. 106-108

4-6 ounces of spaghetti style brown rice noodles

1. Cook chicken and set aside to cool. Cook noodles according to the package directions and rinse with cool water and toss with a touch of oil to prevent sticking. Set aside. Make the dips and prepare the vegetables.

2. On a large platter, arrange all of the ingredients in separate groups. Serve with the following dips (in individual ramekins), allowing everyone to make their own lettuce wraps as desired.

Peanut Sauce

1/2 cup of smooth peanut butter (I use freshly ground, easily found at many grocery stores)

1/3 cup of full fat coconut milk

2 tablespoons naturally fermented soy sauce or tamari (gluten free)

1/8 to 1/4 teaspoon cayenne pepper

3 garlic cloves, peeled and minced

3-4 tablespoons fresh lime juice

Put all of the ingredients into a blender and blend until quite smooth. Thin with water if needed. (Add about a 1/2 tablespoon of fresh ginger, for more punch, if desired.)

Lime Honey Sauce

You may want to double this recipe if you are a lover of lime, as I am.

1/4 cup of fresh lime juice

2 tablespoons honey, preferably raw (heated in a small pan until just liquefied if needed)

1/2 teaspoon salt

2 tablespoons of extra virgin olive oil

Dash or two of cayenne pepper, if desired.

Put all of the ingredients in a small jar and shake vigorously to combine or whisk together in a small bowl.

Chicken & Peach Wraps

We love this flavor combination both in the salad version and in the lettuce wrap version. The wrap allows the chicken and peach flavor to be more concentrated, the lettuce acting as a carrier for the flavorful filling.

* * * 2-4 SERVINGS * * *

Desired lettuce for lettuce cups or wraps (bibb,
  butter, radicchio, endive)
1/2 sweet onion, peeled and chopped
4 small or 2 extra large peaches *pears*
1 recipe of Roasted Chicken Breast or Sautéed
  Chicken, pp. 106-108
1 cup of walnuts
About 1/2 cup of Sweet Onion Poppyseed
Dressing, p. 122

1. In a dry pan over medium high heat, toast the walnuts until they are browned and fragrant, stirring as needed for even browning. Remove to a plate to cool. Chop into smaller pieces (about 1/2 inch pieces).

2. Pit and cut the peaches into bite-sized cubes.

3. In a medium serving bowl combine the peaches, walnuts, onions, and chicken. Toss with enough dressing to coat. Serve with lettuce.

Alternative Dressing:
Strawberry Vinaigrette, p. 121

To Pit and Dice a Peach
With a sharp paring knife, cut around the peach vertically in a complete circle. Gently twist to separate the two halves. Remove the pit and dice into bite-sized pieces.
Sometimes with a very soft and ripe peach, it will resist being twisted to separate. In that case, I slice the peach directly to the pit, pull off each individual slice, then chop into bite sized pieces.

Everyday Lettuce Wraps

You can use everyday sandwich filling ingredients in a lettuce wrap, whether it's tuna fish filling or lunch meat with some vegetables. Here are several ideas and suggestions for fillings. As you can see, the combination options are limitless. Serve with a favorite salad dressing on the side as a dip.

Meats
Sliced Juicy Grassfed Steak, p. 104
Roasted Chicken Breast, p. 106
Sautéed Chicken, p. 108
Nitrate Free Lunch Meat
Applegate Sliced Salami or Pepperoni
Simple Chicken or Tuna Salad*

Cheese
Thinly sliced Cheddar Cheese, Provolone, or Swiss Cheese.
Crumbled Blue Cheese, Gorgonzola, Feta, or Goat Cheese

Vegetables
Sliced Olives
Sliced Avocado
Sliced Red Bell Pepper
Sliced Cucumber
Sliced or Diced Onions

Dressing Suggestions
Everyday Salad Dressing, p. 118
Sweet Apple Cider Vinaigrette, p. 121
Simple Balsamic Vinaigrette, p. 118
Creamy Mexican Avocado Dressing, p. 122

Simple Chicken or Tuna Salad: Combine canned tuna or shredded chicken with a dab of mayonnaise, a squirt of mustard, a spoonful of pickle relish, and chopped celery, if desired. Salt and Pepper to taste.
- OR -
Mix shredded chicken or canned tuna with chopped celery, chopped and toasted nuts of choice, and your favorite vinaigrette.

Choose one meat option, desired cheese, and desired vegetables. Serve with lettuce to wrap in, such as bibb or butterleaf. Dip in ramekins of dressing.

I love bringing these along on trips to the zoo or other outings. Although one time a man noticed me handing rolled lettuce wraps to my 4 year old. He was a little concerned with my choice of lunch for her, as he thought it didn't contain anything inside and I was feeding her just lettuce for lunch! (He also apparently didn't notice the chips on the picnic table.)

Fruit Salads

Melon & Strawberry Salad with Basil Honey Syrup

Cinnamon Vanilla Yogurt Fruit Salad

Mint Fruit Salad

Peaches & Berries with Cream

Creamy Tropical Fruit Salad

Retro Berry Gelatin

In some ways I approached this section with conflicting thoughts. Who really needs to be told how to make a fruit salad? Some of the most delightful fruit salads I've enjoyed have been a very simple concept: ripe fruit chopped into bite sized pieces and served in a pretty bowl; you certainly don't need to be told how to make that!

But sometimes we want just a little more zip. That is where some of my recipes, using a simple honey syrup steeped with mint or basil, can give a subtle flavor that's both elegant and fun. The creamy yogurt and coconut fruit salads are both delicious as well.

You may notice that I often favor a simple two fruit combination. While I love fruit salads full of a wide variety of fruit, when working with seasonal fruit it's often easier, and truthfully, more elegant, to serve a two fruit combination. Strawberries and melon, and peaches and berries, just two examples of this concept, are both pretty and tasty.

Finally, I couldn't resist doing a remix of the Jello salads so (in)famous in our country. Here I use real juice, real flavors, and no refined sugar. There is no need to rely on dyes and sugar found in little boxes on store shelves when there is so much to be found in the produce section.

Melon & Strawberry Salad with Basil Simple Syrup

Melon and strawberries are subtly flavored with basil in this salad. For a real basil punch, you could add some chopped basil to the mix, but I prefer to keep it subtle.

* * * 8 ONE CUP SERVINGS * * *

4-6 cups of diced melon of choice (1 smallish
   honeydew, canteloupe or similar melon)
About 2 cups of sliced fresh strawberries

1/4 cup of honey
1/4 cup of water
Large handful of fresh basil (about 1 cup)

1. Combine the honey and water in a small pot and bring to a simmer. Simmer for one minute, or until the honey is completely dissolved. Take off of the heat and add the basil. Let steep for at least 30 minutes. Strain, and squeeze the basil to get all of the syrup out.

2. Combine the melon and strawberries in a serving bowl and gently toss with the simple syrup. Serve right away.

Melon is a "high volume" food, meaning that for its weight it contains a low amount of calories and a high amount of water, fiber and air. This means it fills you up without requiring you to consume a high amount of calories. It's also full of potassium and vitamin A!

Strawberries are a source of ellagic acid, which has anticarcinogenic and antimutagenic properties (in other words, anti-cancer properties).

93

Cinnamon Vanilla Yogurt Fruit Salad

This fruit salad is good year round, but it's especially nice in the fall and winter, since fall and winter produce, such as apples and oranges, go the very best with the vanilla and cinnamon spiked yogurt sauce. I also like this made with coconut milk yogurt. If you buy store bought coconut milk yogurt, you may not need all of the sweetener, as it's already sweetened.

* * * 8 ONE CUP SERVINGS * * *

1 cup of whole milk yogurt, or coconut milk yogurt.
1 teaspoon powdered cinnamon
1 teaspoon vanilla extract
2 tablespoons honey, preferably raw
8 cups of chopped fruit (one simple combination is apples, oranges, and bananas)
1 cup of walnuts

1. In a small saucepan over medium high heat, toast the walnuts until browned and fragrant. Remove from pan and cool. Chop into 1/2 inch pieces.

2. Combine the yogurt with the cinnamon, vanilla and honey. If the honey is solid, heat until just liquefied in the pan you used for the walnuts. Whisk to combine well.

3. In a serving bowl, combine the fruit, yogurt sauce and nuts. Serve right away, or chill for a couple of hours. If making ahead of time, add bananas right before serving.

An apple a day keeps the doctor away? Apples actually do bring many fascinating benefits, still being studied. For example, they are a source of quercetin, a flavonoid that may help prevent the growth of prostate cancer cells (as studied in a Mayo Clinic study). Cornell University did a study that showed that phtyochemicals from the skin of an apple slowed the reproduction of colon cancer cells by 43%. In the follow up study to the Nurses' Health Study (involving 34,467 women), those who consumed at least one serving of apples and pears per day had a reduced risk of lung cancer.

✳ Mint Fruit Salad

A simple syrup made out of honey is steeped with fresh mint. This makes a refreshing summer fruit salad. You can vary the fruit based on preference and availability. This is another recipe that works well with more common fruit, such as apples, bananas, oranges, grapes, or canteloupe. The optional chopped mint is for mint lovers.

* * * 8 ONE CUP SERVINGS * * *

I/4 cup of water
I/4 honey
I cup of fresh mint leaves (a good handful)

8 cups of fresh fruit, cut into bite sized pieces (such as apples, bananas, oranges, canteloupe, or grapes); if using bananas, add right before serving
I/2 cup of fresh mint, chopped, optional

1. In a small pan, heat the water and honey until simmering. Simmer for one minute, or until the honey has completely dissolved. Remove from heat, add the mint leaves and steep for 30 minutes to 2 hours. (The longer you steep, the more flavor will be released). When the steeping is done, remove leaves with a fork, or pour through a strainer. Squeeze leaves to remove all of the flavorful syrup.

2. In a serving bowl, combine the fruit with the optional mint leaves and toss with the simple syrup. Serve right away.

Oranges are known for their vitamin C content, but they also contain a wide variety of cancer fighting phytochemicals and flavonoids.

Bananas are a good source of potassium. Consumption of bananas has been linked to low rates of kidney cancer. It is also one of the best sources of fructooligosaccharides, which acts as a food for the good bacteria in your body.

Peaches & Berries with Cream

Because simple can be divine. This is perfect for a midsummer light dessert or a bright breakfast. Peaches and berries make a happy marriage. When in the height of the season, they don't need anything at all (though a touch of cream doesn't hurt). If you find your fruit not quite sweet enough, glaze with a bit of simple syrup and let sit for a couple of hours.

* * * 6 SERVINGS * * *

6 large peaches, washed
1 to 2 cups of blackberries or blueberries, washed
Cream or coconut milk

1. Slice peaches by using a small paring knife and slicing right to the center pit of each peach, gently prying the slices off. Place in a large bowl with the berries.

2. Serve with a small pitcher of cream and let people help themselves to both the fruit and the cream.

Simple Honey Syrup
1/4 cup water
1/4 cup honey

In a small pot, combine water and honey. Bring to a simmer and simmer for 1 minute, or until the honey is completely dissolved. Cool.

Blueberries have one of the highest ORAC values of any food. ORAC stands for oxygen radical absorbance capacity, which is a rating system for antioxidant value. Blueberies are also a "memory" food. Dr. James Joseph at the USDA Human Nutrition Research Center found that lab animals fed extracts of blueberry would escape mental deterioration and loss of coordination and balance.

The Department of Nutrition from the University of Oslo in Norway found that blackberries had an even higher amount of antioxidants.

✳ Creamy Tropical Fruit Salad

Tropical fruit is tossed with toasted coconut and a creamy coconut cashew honey dressing. Mild and sweet, this creamy salad is a hit with young people as well as adults. The sauce is also nice with any fruit. You do need to soak the cashews for at least one hour, so keep that in mind when planning to make this recipe.

* * * 8 ONE CUP SERVINGS * * *

8 cups of tropical fruit cut into bite sized pieces
(my favorite combination is 1 pineapple,
  2 bananas, 1 large mango, and 2-4 oranges)
1/2 cup of medium or large unsweetened coconut
  flakes
1/2 cup of raw cashews, soaked 1-4 hours in water,
  then drained and rinsed
1/2 cup of canned full fat coconut milk
2 tablespoons honey, preferably raw
1 1/2 teaspoons lime zest
2 tablespoons freshly squeezed lime juice
Dash of unrefined sea salt

1. In a food processor or powerful blender, add the cashews, coconut milk, honey, lime juice, and salt. Blend until creamy and smooth (about 2 minutes).

2. Toast coconut in a dry pan over medium high heat until toasty brown, stirring to evenly toast (watch carefully, so as to not burn). Cool.

3. Combine the fruit in a serving bowl and toss with the creamy sauce. Chill and sprinkle with the coconut flakes right before serving. Can be made the day before. (If using bananas, I like to add them right before serving for better texture and appearance.)

✳ Mangoes are a source of potassium, vitamin A, vitamin C, vitamin K, calcium, phosphorus and magnesium. They are are also believed to be a good source of enzymes.

✳ Pineapple contains bromelain, a rich source of enzymes that can help with your digestion, speed wound healing, and reduce inflammation. It's also a natural blood thinner. One cup of fresh pineapple gives you 100% of your daily manganese, an essential trace mineral needed for healthy skin, bone, and cartilage.

short bread crust

✳ Retro Berry Gelatin

This recipe has a salty and sweet nut crumb crust and a creamy yogurt filling, topped with a fruit juice based gelatin. It's quite delicious and very sweet. I consider it a dessert. When I was growing up, my mother would make our family a variety of Jello salads. Now that I am a mom myself, I love serving gelatin salads that are based off of those older recipes, but updated with more natural ingredients. No need to reach for a box full of dyes and sugars.

* * * 12-16 SQUARES * * *

2 cups of whole almonds

3 tablespoons coconut oil or butter

3 tablespoons honey, preferably raw

1/2 teaspoon unrefined salt

1 cup of whole milk yogurt (or coconut milk yogurt)

2 tablespoons honey, preferably raw

3 cups of 100% juice, berry flavored (I like Santa Cruz Organic Berry Nectar)

3 tablespoons of honey

1 tablespoon plus 2 teaspoons of gelatin

1 cup of fresh or frozen berries, such as blueberries, raspberries, blackberries, or strawberries, washed if fresh

2 bananas, peeled and thinly sliced

Grease a square pan (8 by 8 or 9 by 9)

1. In a large saucepan, toast the whole almonds over medium high heat until lightly browned, stirring as needed to prevent burning and promote even browning.

2. Place in a food processor with the coconut oil or butter, and 3 tablespoons of honey and salt. Process until finely ground with a crumb like texture (it should hold together when a spoonful of it is pressed together). Press into the bottom of the pan evenly.

3. Mix the yogurt and 2 tablespoons of honey together. If needed, heat the honey until just liquefied before adding to the yogurt. Spread evenly over the nut mixture.

4. Place 1 cup of the juice in a medium sized bowl. Sprinkle the gelatin over the top of the juice and gently mix in to moisten all of it. Set aside to soften. In a small pot, add 1 cup of the juice and 3 tablespoons of honey and heat until it reaches a simmer. Carefully pour into the gelatin and juice mixture and stir to dissolve the gelatin. Add the rest of the juice and fruit. Ladle over the yogurt mixture (some of the yogurt mixture will mix in, but that's okay).

5. Place in the refrigerator to set (it will take at least 3-4 hours). I've also speed up the process by placing it in the freezer for about 1 1/2 hours.

6. Cut into squares and serve.

Steak, Chicken, & Other Good Stuff

Juicy Grassfed Steak

Mexican Beef

Roasted Chicken Breast

Sauteed Chicken Breast

Herbed Garlic Croutons

Mary's Oil Blend

Homemade Mayonnaise

Cinnamon & Vanilla Candied Nuts

Slow Roasted Salmon

Homemade Beans

Juicy Grassfed Steak

I am in love with this method of cooking grassfed steak. It comes out juicy, tender and delicious. You don't want to overexpose the steak to high heat as it will cause the better muscle tone of the grassfed meat to become chewy and dry. So we start with high heat, and finish with low heat. The result is a delicious juicy steak. (My thanks to Shannon Hayes, author of "The Farmer and the Grill" and several other cookbooks designed for grassfed beef, for pointing me in the right direction.) This makes a nice steak on the side of a large salad. Or, slice a sirloin steak to serve in the salad itself.

* * *

Unrefined salt, freshly ground pepper

2 tablespoons ghee, Mary's Oil Blend, p. 110, or butter

1 sirloin, sirloin tip, tri-tip, top round or London Broil, rib eye, porterhouse, t-bone, top loin (NY Strip) or tenderloin (filet mignon) steak, 1 inch or thicker (if using a really long steak, cut in half to better fit in the pan, if needed)

1. Pat the steak dry and season well with salt and pepper. Leave to bring to room temperature.

2. Preheat the oven to 200 degrees Fahrenheit. Turn on the oven fan, as this is going to get smoky. Heat a heavy, oven safe pan, such as a cast iron, over medium high heat until just starting to smoke. Add the fat of choice to the pan, and then the steak. Cook, without disturbing for 2-3 minutes on each side. Stick an instant read thermometer in the side of the steak and place the pan in the oven until the temperature reaches 135 to 155 degrees. This will take anywhere between 5 minutes to 20, depending on the thickness of the steak.

3. Remove from pan and dab with butter. Let sit for at least 5 minutes before serving or slicing.

Grassfed beef is not as fatty as grain finished beef. This means that you need a slightly different technique to properly cook it. The effort is worth it because grassfed beef is higher nutritionally across the board. It has higher omega 3 fatty acids, more vitamin E, and more beta-carotene. It also has much higher CLA content, which has a host of benefits, as mentioned in the introduction to this book.

Mexican Beef

This recipe is surprisingly simple. With just a few seasonings I keep in the cupboard, fresh garlic, and a lime, I create a wholesome Mexican beef. This is in contrast to the seasoning packets you can buy at the store, which are full of unfortunate ingredients (just look below for an example). I was thrilled that my simple recipe was very well received by my recipe testers. It proved to me once again that simple food can be popular.

* * *

1 pound of beef, preferably 100% grassfed
1 teaspoon each of ground cumin and dried
   oregano
3 cloves of garlic, peeled and finely minced or
   put through a garlic press
1/8 to 1/4 teaspoon of cayenne pepper
Unrefined salt to taste
Juice from 1 lime

1. Combine the meat, cumin, oregano, garlic, and cayenne in a large saucepan. Cook over medium high heat, stirring to cook evenly, until the meat is completely cooked through. When using grassfed beef, you shouldn't have any grease to drain. If you do, push all of the meat to one side of the pan and tip the pan to pool the grease in one side of the pan. Remove the grease with a spoon.

2. Sprinkle the lime juice over the meat and salt to taste.

Contrast this recipe to the ingredients in a popular Mexican seasoning packet: "Corn Starch, Maltodextrin, Hydrolyzed Corn and Soy Protein, Sugar, Salt, Chili Pepper, Spice, Onion Powder, Garlic Powder, Citric Acid, Artificial Color, Silicon Dioxide (Anticaking Agent), Partially Hydrogenated Soybean Oil, Natural Smoke Flavor, Sulfiting Agents, Ethoxyquin (Preservatives)"

Roasted Chicken Breast

If you roast chicken on the bone with the skin intact, you will end up with chicken that is much more tender and tasty. I also keep the bones to make soup stock (find the recipe on my blog, thenourishinggourmet.com), which stretches my food budget even further. If you want a faster recipe, turn the page for sautéed chicken breast or thighs, where you do use boneless, skinless chicken pieces and you can have it ready to eat within 15 minutes. This roasted chicken recipe is exceedingly simple, yet quite good.

* * *

2 chicken breasts on the bone (about 1 1/2 to 2 pounds)
About 2 tablespoons of Mary's Oil Blend, p. 110, melted butter, coconut oil or olive oil
Unrefined salt and freshly ground pepper

1. Preheat the oven to 375 degrees Fahrenheit. Place the chicken breast in a pie pan or other small pan. Brush the top with the fat of choice. Salt and pepper liberally.

2. Place in the oven and cook for 45 minutes, or until the juices run clear when pierced with a knife and/or the internal temperature reaches 165 degrees.

3. Remove and let sit for ten minutes. Slice off the bone and shred or cube to use in a salad recipe.

You can also use chicken legs in this recipe, but you will have to shred the chicken off the bone rather than cube it. It isn't quite as pretty, but I actually love the taste of dark meat and it's definitely more frugal.

✳ Sautéed Chicken Breast or Thighs

This one works great for getting food on the table fast (the roasted chicken recipe is delicious, but does require a long time in the oven). I also like to use this recipe in the summertime, when I don't want my oven on for 45 minutes. Like the roasted chicken recipe, this one is simple, with simple seasonings.

* * *

1 pound of boneless, skinless chicken breast or thighs
2 tablespoons of fat of choice (Mary's Oil Blend, p. 110, coconut oil, olive oil or combination of olive oil and butter)

1. Cut raw chicken into bite sized pieces

2. In a large pan, heat fat of choice over medium high heat. When the pan is hot, but not smoking, add the chicken and sprinkle with salt and pepper. Cook until the chicken is cooked all the way through and remove from pan. Or cook whole pieces until done, let stand on cutting board for 5 minutes + cut into bite size pieces. More moist + tasty - seasonings more even.

✳ Chicken meat is a great source of high quality protein as well as a good source of phosphorus, potassium and vitamin B's, like niacin. Protein provides the amino acids our bodies need to balance hormones, repair and keep us in good shape.

Herbed Garlic Croutons

*Two slices of bread can be transformed into crunchy croutons for
a delightful addition to salads. I've had success using gluten free bread in this
recipe, as well as whole grain sourdough and sprouted whole wheat bread.*

* * *

2 slices of whole grain bread, cubed, crust cut off
   if desired
2 tablespoons each of olive oil and butter, or 4
   tablespoons Mary's Oil Blend, p. 110
3 garlic cloves, crushed and peeled, optional
2 teaspoons dried rosemary, optional
Salt and pepper

1. In a large saucepan, heat the olive oil and butter until hot
(but never smoking).

2. Add the bread, garlic (keep crushed, don't mince) and
rosemary, sprinkle with salt and pepper. You can either brown
on one side, and then flip over to brown on the other side,
or you can gently stir as it cooks to evenly brown. Cook until
the bread is browned and getting crunchy. Take out the garlic
cloves early if they brown faster than the bread.

3. Remove from heat and cool.

Store bought croutons are most
often full of rancid, refined, omega
6 rich oils, preservatives, and sta-
bilizers. Homemade croutons only
take a few minutes to make, and you
completely control the quality. They
certainly taste better, too; a world
apart from store bought!

*toast 1 slice bread
when nice + browned
spread with soft butter.
Cut into strips one way)
turn + cut strips into
cubes.*

Mary's Oil Blend

This simple oil blend was suggested by Mary Enig in the book, Eat Fat, Lose Fat. It allows you to experience the benefits of coconut oil and sesame oil without having to use either of them exclusively. You can use this oil blend in the salad dressing recipes, or use it when sautéing. It has a more mellow flavor than the bite of many olive oils, with a slightly nutty taste from the sesame seed oil, and a bit of a sweetness from the coconut oil. I do taste the coconut oil when I use this oil blend in recipes, so if you think that will bother you, be aware. It's suggested in the book, Eat Fat, Lose Fat, that this oil blend is a better one to use when trying to lose weight.

* * *

1 cup of expeller pressed, or cold pressed sesame oil (unrefined and not toasted)
1 cup of unrefined coconut oil
1 cup of extra virgin olive oil.

1. Melt the coconut oil in a small saucepan on low heat until the oil is just melted (on a hot day, your oil will already be liquefied and you can skip this step).

2. Mix in with the other two oils. Keep at room temperature.

You can make this in any quantity you want.

Sesame oil is very high in antioxidants which is one reason why sesame seed oil doesn't go rancid for a very long time. It also may help lower cholesterol and blood pressure. However, it is high in omega 6 fatty-acids, so you shouldn't use it exclusively.

Coconut oil is a powerhouse of benefits because it contains M.C.T.'s (medium-chain triglycerides). The predominant M.C.T. is lauric acid, which is found in only a few foods, mother's milk being one, coconut oil another. M.C.T.'s have been found to fight a wide variety of bad bacteria without having a negative effect on good bacteria.

Homemade Mayonnaise   *tofu w/page 118*

Mayonnaise can be a little tricky, but with a few tips, you can successfully make your own at home. First, use fresh eggs. The lecithin in eggs is crucial to the process, and the lecithin in older eggs breaks down. Second, the type of oil you choose to make your mayonnaise with will definitely influence the flavor. Originally, mayonnaise was made with olive oil, which has a bite to it. We are used to almost flavorless mayonnaise. Using a very mild olive oil will give you a milder olive oil flavor. Using Mary's Oil Blend will give a mild, but kind of sweet and nutty taste to your mayonnaise. My current favorite is using a combination of mild olive oil and macadamia oil.

* * *

1-2 egg yolks

1 teaspoon mustard (yellow or brown)

2 teaspoons of fresh lemon juice

1/2 teaspoon unrefined salt

3/4- 1 cup of very mild extra virgin olive oil, Mary's Oil Blend, p. 110, expeller pressed macadamia nut oil, or combination of olive oil and expeller pressed macadamia oil

Hand Blender Version

In a tall container just large enough for the stick blender (such as the container most hand blenders come with), add the egg yolks, mustard, salt, and lemon juice. Blend until combined, then with the blender on, slowly add the oil and watch as it thickens right before your eyes. Blend until all of the oil is just incorporated. You can thin out with warm water or lemon juice, if desired. Keeps 3-7 days

Food Processor or Blender Method

Combine the egg yolks, mustard, lemon juice, and salt in a food processor with a blade or regular blender. Blend. Then with the machine on, slowly add the oil until just combined and thick. Overbeaten olive oil can end up bitter, so I recommend Mary's oil blend with this method. You can thin out with warm water or lemon juice, if desired. Keeps 3-7 days.

If your mayonnaise breaks and ends up looking like egg drop soup, scrape the mixture into bowl. Clean out the container. Add a fresh egg yolk. Blend, then add spoonful by spoonful of broken mixture into the egg yolk, blending as before, until you've mixed in all of the broken mixture. Then you can add the rest of the oil.

Unfortunately, most storebought mayonnaise is made with inferior oils and ingredients, making them a poor choice to use on a regular basis. Making your own solves that problem. Look at the Resource Section (page 124-125) for some options when buying.

However, you do have to be comfortable consuming raw egg when making your own. I do not recommend using "factory" produced eggs, but only local, pastured eggs, and always re-washing the shell before cracking.

Cinnamon & Vanilla Candied Nuts

Not too sweet, and laced with cinnamon and vanilla, these nuts were an instant hit at my house and on my website as well. Add to either fruit salads or green salads for a sweet treat.

* * *

1 egg white
2 teaspoons of cinnamon
1 teaspoon of vanilla extract
1 teaspoon of salt
1/3 cup of rapadura, sucanat, maple sugar, or
   palm/coconut sugar
2 1/2 cups of walnuts (or nut of choice, such as
   pecans, cashews, etc)

1. Preheat the oven to 300 degrees Fahrenheit with the rack in the middle of the oven. Lightly coat a cookie pan with coconut oil or butter, or cover with parchment paper.

2. Lightly heat the egg white with a whisk (just until a bit foamy). Add the cinnamon, vanilla, salt and sugar. Fold in the walnuts, coating well.

3. Remove the walnuts with a slotted spoon (allowing extra coating to drip out), and place on the cookie sheet. Spread out on the cookie sheet so that the nuts aren't touching for the most part. Place in the oven for 25 minutes.

4. Remove from the oven and cool for 20 minutes. Serve or store in an airtight container for up to two weeks.

These nuts also make great gifts. Make a double or triple batch and package up in small jars or tins. Homemade candied nuts are always a special treat, and it's nice to share that love.

Slow Roasted Salmon

"Slow" only means about 20 minutes, but by cooking at a low temperature, all of the juices are locked in for very flavorful and moist salmon. The other advantage to slow roasting your salmon? It's almost impossible to overcook at such a low temperature. I've left direct amounts off this recipe, as you can easily make this with either 6 ounces or 36 ounces of fish.

* * *

Center cut, boneless, skin on salmon, room temperature
Drizzle of extra virgin olive oil
Unrefined salt and pepper

Preheat the oven to 275 degrees Fahrenheit

1. Place salmon, skin side down, in a pie pan or other small pan. Drizzle a little olive oil over it. Lightly salt and pepper.

2. Cook for 20-25 minutes, or until the salmon is cooked all the way through. To test for doneness, stick a sharp paring knife in the thickest part. If it cuts through very easily, it's done.

I recommend buying Alaskan wild salmon because it's the purest and highest quality. Salmon is an amazing food, full of omega 3 fatty-acids, and high in protein, too. It's one of the best foods we can eat, in my opinion!

If you are used to cooking fish until it's dry, this recipe will take some getting used to, as it remains quite soft and moist. But that's just why it's so delicious. No one likes a dried out piece of fish.

✳ *Homemade Beans*

*Cooking your own beans, rather than buying canned, saves a significant amount of money. It's also quite
simple to do. It just takes a bit of time on the stove. I do long soaks when I cook beans, as I believe it makes
them more digestible. I also like to cook beans with kombu, a seaweed, because it adds more minerals to the beans
as well as making them more digestible and tasty. Leave it out, if desired. By soaking for long periods of time in
warm water, you also reduce some of the anti-nutrients present in beans, such as phytic acid. Phytic acid
prevents you from absorbing nutrients, so beans will be more nutritious when soaked.*

* * *

**2 cups of beans (or amount desired; 1 cup of
   dried beans makes about 3 cups of cooked)**
Plenty of water (preferably filtered)
1 long strip of kombu

1. In a large pot, put the beans and add plenty of warm
water to cover (you want the water level to be several
inches above the beans). Remove any beans that float on
the surface of the water. Let soak in a warm place for 12-
24 hours. Drain and rinse well.

2. Add the beans back to the pot and cover with new water and kombu strip, if using. Bring to a very low simmer,
skim any scum that comes to the surface, and simmer
until the beans are soft (see cooking times below). Drain
to use in recipes, and remove kombu. Save liquid for
freezing beans.

Approximate Cooking Times for Soaked Beans:
Black Beans: 1 to 1 1/2 hours, Most White Beans: 1 to 1 1/2
hours, Garbanzo Beans: 1 to 2 hours.

Notes:
Cooking times will vary according to how old the beans
are and how long you soaked them. I've had beans cook

in about 45 minutes, but I've also had beans that never
cooked correctly, as they were too old. Your best bet is to
buy your beans from a store with a good turnaround.

To add flavor, you can add herbs to the beans as they
cook, such as a bay leaf or two, sprigs of rosemary or
thyme, or cloves of garlic, peeled.

To make the beans' texture even more smooth, you can
add a couple of tablespoons of olive oil, ghee, or fat of
choice to the cooking water.

Some cooks add salt at the beginning of the cooking
time, some do in the middle, and some at the end, when
the beans are all the way cooked. It has been long believed that salt would make the beans stay hard and not
completely soften, when added during the cooking process. That is now believed to be erroneous, but I've had
a few pots of beans never soften when cooked in salted
water, so I stay on the conservative side, and salt after
they are cooked.

To freeze, separate the beans into 2 cup portions and
then cover with reserved cooking liquid. Freeze for 2-3
months.

Salad Dressings

Everyday Salad Dressing

Simple Balsamic Vinaigrette

Lemon Pepper Dressing

Caesar Dressing

Roasted Garlic Dressing

Sweet Apple Cider Vinaigrette

Strawberry Vinaigrette

Sweet Onion Poppyseed Dressing

Creamy Mexican Avocado Dressing

Mexican Vinaigrette

tofu mayo base
Don't over blend oil (turns bitter)

Everyday Salad Dressing

I make large batches of this salad dressing and use it for a wide variety of dishes. It's one of our favorites and very multi-purpose. I've used and enjoyed it for years now.

* * * Yield: 1 1/3 cups * * *

1/4 cup rice vinegar

- ~~1/3 cup of raw apple cider vinegar~~
- 1 cup of extra virgin olive oil
- 2 tablespoons prepared mustard (Eden's organic brown mustard or a Dijon style mustard)
- 3 smallish garlic cloves, peeled and finely minced or put through a garlic press
- 1/2 teaspoon each of dried thyme and basil
- 1 1/2 teaspoons salt *celery seed*

Combine ingredients in a Mason jar with a plastic storing lid and shake vigorously to combine. Or, whisk in a small bowl and place in a container to store.

Variations:

Lightly Sweetened: Add 2 teaspoons to 2 tablespoons of honey (to taste) to tame the tang.

With Anchovies: For added flavor and nutrition blend 3 anchovies with the apple cider vinegar in a blender until smooth. Remove from blender and combine with the rest of the ingredients.

Simple Balsamic Vinaigrette

see page 121

Balsamic vinegar is both sweet and tangy. The longer it's been aged the more concentrated and sweet it becomes. I find that vinegars aged for 10 plus years can be a little too sweet for me, so I use balsamic vinegar aged for 3-5. This dressing is another good one to double or triple to keep on hand.

* * * Yield: 1 cup * * *

- 1/4 cup of balsamic vinegar
- 3/4 cup of extra virgin olive oil
- 2-4 teaspoons high quality brown mustard (Eden's organic brown mustard or a Dijon style mustard)
- 1-3 garlic clove, finely minced or put through a garlic press
- 3/4 teaspoon salt

Combine ingredients in a Mason jar with a plastic storing lid and shake vigorously to combine. Or whisk in a small bowl and place in a container to store.

Variations:

With Shallots: Add 1/4 cup of finely chopped shallots.

Lemon Pepper Dressing

This is another dressing that I use often in a variety of salads. The lemon zest brings more lemon flavor to the dressing. The pepper sounds like a lot, but the dressing is quite mild.

* * * Yield: 1 cup * * *

3/4 cup of extra virgin olive oil
1/4 cup of freshly squeezed lemon juice
1 tablespoon ground pepper, preferably freshly ground
1 teaspoon lemon zest (from lemon used for juice)
1 teaspoon unrefined salt

Combine ingredients in a Mason jar with a plastic storing lid and shake vigorously to combine. Or, whisk in a small bowl and place in a container to store.

Variations:

With Garlic: Add 1 to 3 garlic cloves, peeled and finely minced or put through a garlic press.

With Dried Basil or Oregano: Add 1 teaspoon of dried basil or oregano.

Caesar Dressing

Creamy, tangy, and full of nourishing ingredients, this is a great favorite. You really can use this beyond Caesar salad, so get creative and enjoy this salad dressing often! My husband likes this dressing on the salty side, so I add the optional salt.

* * * Yield: About 1 1/2 cups * * *

6 anchovy fillets canned in oil (I look for ones canned in glass jars. Keep the extras in the refrigerator or freezer.)
3 garlic cloves, peeled and roughly chopped
1 egg yolk *
1 tablespoon brown mustard (Eden's organic brown mustard or a Dijon style mustard)
2 tablespoons each of raw apple cider vinegar and balsamic vinegar
1/2 cup of freshly grated Parmesan
3/4 cup of olive oil
1/2 teaspoon unrefined salt, optional

1. In a food processor or blender, blend the anchovy fillets, garlic cloves, mustard, vinegar, Parmesan, and salt until smooth (scrape down the sides as needed).
2. Add the olive oil and blend briefly to combine. Best served day of, but will keep up to three days refrigerated.

* This does use a raw egg yolk, so I only use high quality, pastured eggs in this recipe, and I always wash the outside of the egg before cracking. You can also use the egg yolk from a soft or hard-boiled egg, though the texture won't be quite as smooth. You can leave the egg yolk out entirely, but it won't have quite the same texture.

Roasted Garlic Dressing

When garlic is roasted, it is tamed into a sweet mild flavor. While this recipe contains four whole heads of garlic, a common comment is that the garlic flavor is very mild. For the garlic lovers, you may want to try the "double garlic version" which has the punch of the raw garlic as well as the mild creaminess of the roasted garlic. This also makes a great dairy free alternative to Caesar salad dressing.

* * * *Yield: About 1 1/2 cups* * * *

4 heads of garlic
A drizzle of olive oil
Unrefined Salt
1/4 cup of raw apple cider vinegar plus two
   tablespoons
2 tablespoons of high quality mustard (Eden's
organic brown mustard or a Dijon style mustard)
I teaspoon unrefined salt
3/4 cup of extra virgin mild olive oil

1. Cut off the top 1/4 to 1/2 inch of the garlic (the opposite side of the roots). Drizzle liberally with olive oil and place in a glass pie pan or other small pan. Cover with foil (don't let it touch the garlic to prevent any metal transfer to your food).

2. Cook for I to I 1/2 hours or until the garlic is very soft when pierced with a knife. Allow to cool.

3. In a blender or food processor, add the garlic, peeled. (Gently squeeze the roasted garlic on the root side to remove garlic from the peel. Occasionally, I find that I need to use a spoon to scoop the garlic out.)

4. Add the vinegar, mustard, and salt, then purée until smooth, scraping down the sides as needed.

5. With the blender/food processor on, add the oil until just combined (don't blend beyond this point; otherwise it can make the oil bitter). Pour/scrape into a container and refrigerate if not using right away.

Keeps up to two weeks.

Variation:

Double Garlic: Add 1-3 coarsely chopped raw garlic cloves with the roasted garlic in the blender.

Sweet Apple Cider Vinaigrette

This dressing has lighter flavors. It's sweet, but not overly so. It has an onion and garlic punch, but it's still subtle. There are no herbs to distract you. This is a favorite of my four year old, and has been a family favorite for years (even before I upgraded the recipe with more nourishing ingredients). For this recipe, I prefer a very mild olive oil.

* * * *Yield: 2 cups* * * *

1 large shallot, or about 1/4 cup of chopped red
   onion or sweet onion
1 small clove of garlic
1 tablespoon brown mustard (Eden's Organic
   Brown Mustard or Dijon style mustard)
2 tablespoons honey, preferably raw
1/8 teaspoon unrefined salt
1/2 cup of raw apple cider vinegar
1 1/2 cup of mild olive oil or Mary's Oil Blend,
   p.110

In a blender, add the shallot or onion, garlic, mustard, honey, salt, and vinegar. Blend until smooth. Add the olive oil and blend until just combined.

Lasts 1 month in the refrigerator.

Strawberry Vinaigrette

This dressing is a beauty with it's bright color. It's also absolutely delicious! I haven't tried them yet, but I bet that raspberries and other berries would be great too.

* * * *Yield: About 1 1/2 cups* * * *

1/2 cup of balsamic vinegar
1 pint of strawberries, stemmed and washed
1/2 sweet onion or red onion
1 1/2 teaspoon unrefined salt
4 tablespoons honey, preferably raw
1 cup of mild olive oil or Mary's Oil Blend, p. 110

In a blender or food processor, combine the vinegar, strawberries, onion, salt, and honey. Blend until smooth. Add the olive oil and blend until just combined. Pour into a Mason jar or storing jar.

Lasts 3-5 days, refrigerated.

Sweet Onion Poppyseed Dressing

*This sweet dressing is full of flavor. It's perfect to
serve with green salads that include fruit. You can just
grate the onion, add to the dressing, and whisk to combine,
but the dressing will have the more typical creamy white
color when blended together. Save the other half of the sweet
onion to thinly slice and add to a green salad. Yum!*

* * * *Yield: 1 1/3 cups* * * *

1/2 sweet onion, quartered
1 tablespoon brown mustard (Eden's
    Organic Brown mustard or a Dijon style
    mustard)
1 teaspoon unrefined salt
1/4 to 1/3 cup of honey, preferably raw
1/3 cup of raw apple cider vinegar
3/4 cup of extra virgin olive oil or Mary's Oil
    Blend, p. 110
1 tablespoon poppyseeds

In a blender or food processor, combine the onion, mustard, salt, and vinegar. Blend until smooth. Add the olive
oil and blend until just combined. Pour into a Mason jar
or storing jar, and stir in the poppyseeds.

Keeps up to 2 weeks.

Creamy Mexican Avocado Dressing

*This has to be one of my favorite new dressings.
It's so creamy and flavorful. The larger the avocado, the more
dressing this makes. If you have an extra large salad to dress,
make sure you use a large avocado, or 2 to 3 small ones.*

* * * *Yield: About 1 1/3 cups* * * *

1 large avocado
3 tablespoons of fresh lemon juice
1 teaspoon ground cumin
1 teaspoon unrefined salt
3 garlic cloves, peeled and coarsely chopped
1/2 cup of extra virgin olive oil

In a blender or food processor, blend all of the ingredients except the olive oil, until smooth (about 2 minutes).
Scrape down the sides as needed. Add the olive oil and
blend until just combined. Can make several hours before
serving.

Keeps up to 2 weeks.

✳ *Mexican Vinaigrette*

I enjoy this vinaigrette that is spiced with Mexican fla-
vors. It's perfect for both grain and green salads. I think it
would also work well in a legume based salad.

* * * *Yield: 1 1/3 cups* * * *

3/4 cup of mild olive oil
1/4 cup of raw apple cider vinegar
1 teaspoon ground cumin
1/8 to 1/4 teaspoon cayenne pepper *or chili*
1 teaspoon unrefined salt
1 teaspoon dried oregano
3 garlic cloves, peeled and finely minced or put
through a garlic press

Combine ingredients in a Mason jar with a plastic storing
lid and shake vigorously to combine. Or, whisk in a small
bowl and place in a container to store.

Keeps up to 2 weeks.

Resources

The majority of the ingredients used in this book can be found at most grocery stores, health food stores, and local farmer's markets. However, I did want to direct you to a few brands that I use. Many of these brands can be found in your local store, but I've provided links to the company's website, so that you can read more about the company or products, if desired.

Canned Beans

Eden Organic carries a wide variety of canned beans. They are canned in stainless steel cans with a BPA-free enamel coating. Because the cost of these cans is 14% higher than other cans used in the market, I find them more expensive to buy. I try to keep some on hand for last minute meals, but making homemade beans and freezing them is more frugal. www.edenfoods.com

Canned Seafood

Once again, I recommend using fresh seafood whenever possible, but having canned seafood on hand helps you make last minute salads more easily. Canned Salmon and Tuna (low mercury, BPA free): www.wildplanetfoods.com
Anchovies: www.crownprince.com

Salami

Most salami has nitrates and nonfat milk powder in it; two ingredients I avoid. My local store carries Applegate's salami and we love it! It's gluten and dairy free too, for those with allergies. www.applegatefarms.com

Olive Oil

There are so many good varieties of olive oils, it's hard to decide which ones to list. The one mentioned in my introduction, certainly one of the most mild olive oils I've ever tasted (their late season oil is the mildest), is Chaffin Family Orchard's olive oil.
www.chaffinfamilyorchards.com

I recently found out that there are more local Oregon olive growers that I am planning to look into. I encourage you to try American grown olive oils from farms or companies that source their olive oil from one farm. It ensures better quality control.

Coconut Oil

There is a wide variety of coconut oil brands, almost all of them very good. Here is a short list of some of my favorites:

www.wildernessfamilynaturals.com
www.mountainroseherbs.com (make sure you buy the "unrefined" coconut oil)
www.tropicaltraditions.com
www.nutiva.com

Sesame Oil

Unrefined, Expeller Pressed Sesame Oil:
www.spectrumorganics.com
www.tropicaltraditions.com
www.wildernessfamilynaturals.com
www.napavalleynaturals.com

Toasted Sesame Oil
www.edenfoods.com
www.spectrumorganics.com

Unfiltered, Raw Apple Cider Vinegar
www.bragg.com
www.solanagold.com

Unrefined Sugar
Rapadura: www.tropicaltraditions.com
Sucanat: www.wholesomesweeteners.com
www.sweet-tree.biz
Raw Honey: www.reallyrawhoney.com

Organic Brown Mustard and Kombu
The mustard and kombu that I use both come
from Eden Organic. www.edenfoods.com

Mayonnaise
I recommend making your own (p. 111) when
possible, but here are some brands that are good
substitutes.

Mayonnaise made using Mary's Oil Blend:
www.wildernessfamilynaturals.com
(highly recommended)
Mayonnaise made with sunflower oil:
French Mayonnaise - Delouis Fils (available from
various online stores).

Compromise Brands
Hain's Safflower Mayonnaise
Grapeseed Veganaise: www.followyourheart.com

Unrefined Salt
Celtic Sea Salt: www.celticseasalt.com
Real Salt: www.realsalt.com
Wide Selection of Salts:
www.wildernessfamilynaturals.com
Himalayan Salt:
www.products.mercola.com/himalayan-salt
www.swansonvitamins.com

Salad Bag
My favorite salad bag so far is the Silvermark Microfiber
Salad Bag. It dries and stores the lettuce.

Microfiber Salad Bag: www.silvermk.com

Pickle Relish
Bubbie's pickle relish is not only delicous, but it's also
naturally fermented with no preservatives, vinegars, or
sugar. Highly recommended.
Bubbie's Kosher Pickle Relish: www.bubbies.com

Index

21698169R00069

Made in the USA
Lexington, KY
24 March 2013